RELIGION AND PUBLIC LIFE

Religion and Public Life
Tom Butler's Thoughts For The Day

Tom Butler

continuum

Continuum International Publishing Group

The Tower Building	80 Maiden Lane
11 York Road	Suite 704
London	New York
SE1 7NX	NY 10038

www.continuumbooks.com

First published 2012

British Library Cataloguing-in-Publication Data
A catalogue record for this book is available from the British Library.

ISBN: 978-1441-10177-8 (paperback)

Typeset by Fakenham Prepress Solutions, Fakenham, Norfolk NR21 8NN
Printed and bound in India

Contents

Introduction

'Anyone who wants to live responsibly must read two things, the Bible and the daily newspaper, and never one without the other.' This is what the great Swiss theologian Karl Barth is reported to have advised one of his students. Certainly this book is an attempt to live out that advice. Its Genesis is delving into the 'Thought for the Day' scripts which I have written and presented over 20 years for BBC Radio 4's *Today* programme.

Today is a hard news programme, but it has within it predicable slots for sport, the weather and 'Thought for the Day'. The brief of 'Thought' is to give a theological or spiritual comment on the news of the day. It should be focused on the news or it is difficult to justify the slot being in a hard news programme, but if it does not have a specific theological or spiritual emphasis then it will be adding little value to a news story which is probably being covered thoroughly through interview or comment elsewhere in the programme. Unlike the rest of the programme, 'Thought' has no balancing comeback through somebody contributing a differing view, and so the attempt is made to provide balance within each contribution; not easy in under three minutes without sounding bland! Also, because 'Thought' is always delivered live and is focused on the news, the script cannot be prepared before the previous evening, and then, not infrequently, needs to be adapted as the news develops overnight.

The event usually is quite apparent. It might stem out of a natural disaster, or an international or national decision or development. It might come out of the world of politics, education or science. Something that an individual has said or done might be dominating the news. Because the dates for the presentation are in the diary well in advance, the decision is not to present a 'Thought' because something of great moment is happening; it is to select from the events of that particular day something which is of particular interest, whether dramatic or not.

The challenge is then to select a theological or spiritual approach which will add insight or interest to an audience who may be neither informed or overinterested in religious matters. Sometimes the approach presents itself instantly; at other times there is the rich mine of the Bible, Church history, contemporary Christian voices, or the insights of other religious traditions.

For the purpose of this book I have made a selection from the scripts which I have written and presented over the years and grouped them into particular themes, with a chapter commenting upon each theme. During this time I was successively bishop of Willesden, Leicester and Southwark and hopefully the scripts and commentary will give an indication of the way in which a bishop in the Church of England, working in a variety of environments, has approached issues in public life over an extended period. My previous experience of training as a scientist and working in Central Africa for over five years has probably also influenced my attitudes and interests.

It will become apparent that my general interest has been to explore how the Church can influence, be involved with, and work for, the 'common good'. Some of the scripts refer to global, some to national, some to local, and some to individual issues and this is understandable because the common good might be seen as the total conditions which allow society, groups and individuals to reach fulfilment. This involves respect for individuals, but it also involves paying attention too to the wellbeing of international and national societies and the groups within them, including matters of justice, war and peace. Some of the issues covered have been quite controversial and divisive within Church and state, others less so, but it might be of interest to observe that I did not necessarily choose the most dramatic issues or events within them, for a 'Thought for the Day' attempts to address what happens to be in the news that particular morning and the news is beyond the power of the presenter to control.

When I was preparing for ordination, having previously trained as a scientist, my tutor gave me an essay to write. 'What books should I consult?' I asked him. 'The Bible is very good,' was his reply, and of course it is. All human life is to be found within the pages of its many books written over different centuries in different eras and cultures. Sex, violence, power, slavery, love, hate, war, peace, gentleness and goodness are all there mixed up with a menu of religious faith and faithlessness. It is always a good starting point. Church history is also an encyclopedia of politics, arguments, saints, eccentrics, martyrs and mystics, whilst contemporary Church politics well reflect the machinations of Whitehall or the United Nations, for the Church might see itself as the 'mystical body of Christ', or made up of the 'congregation of faithful believers', but as with other bodies it is also a very human institution, made up of men and women with their foibles and failings. But there are impressive characters also and we can all be challenged by the likes of Mother Theresa or Desmond Tutu.

The Bible and the Church then are rich mines for anyone wishing to seek theological or spiritual insight or warning on contemporary events, but in Britain we are all fortunate in living cheek by jowl with those of different religious faiths and traditions and probably there is no better place on earth, and no better time in history to have access to faith stories and insights other than our own. 'Thought for the Day' presenters come from a variety of faith traditions and it is usually right and proper to leave others to comment from that tradition, but occasionally there is an obvious overlap and I have therefore trespassed into a spiritual tradition not my own, which has brought me new insights on my own tradition.

Then there are contemporary developments which people of whatever faith have not needed to address in the past. We can think in particular of the developments in the medical sciences bringing with them a multitude of new ethical issues. I devote a chapter to these. Then the developments in quantum physics and astronomy are literally mind blowing and often make the most obscure mystical religious insight seem quite straight-forward. I touch upon some of this in the chapter on science.

Again the developments in modern weaponry, with smart bombs and devastation through a technician's finger, make modern warfare a very different animal to that seen by previous generations. The chapter on the Gulf War and its associate chapter on terrorism illustrate a further factor in producing a 'Thought'. Each presentation is an instant reaction to a snapshot of the news of the day without the benefit of knowing how the news will develop or what the eventual outcome will be. We now know, of course, the messy outcome in Iraq of the two Gulf wars but when each script was presented we did not know. A vivid example of this is the presentation 'Crossing the Rubicon', given during the Second Gulf War in April 2003, for that was the day that US soldiers would be crossing the border of Baghdad. We did not know at that time whether or not the Iraqis had chemical weapons but if they had they would surely have used them on US personnel that day. We now know that the soldiers were not at that kind of risk but revisiting the script is a reminder of the drama and the doubt of the times. I also have found it illuminating to see how my mind and attitude – no doubt reflecting that of the average Radio 4 listener – have solidified or changed over the 20 years time span and the different or common religious resources which have been drawn upon.

The basic theological understanding, however, has not changed: the belief in a Creator God with the consequence that creation and the science which seeks to understand its workings matters and is susceptible to rational thought; the belief in Jesus Christ who was incarnated as Jesus of Nazareth with the consequence that humanity supremely matters because God has shared and understands its life; the belief in the Holy Spirit which is ever leading us into new truth as we come to understand more about our world and ourselves. A consequence of all of this is my belief that we can gain understanding of the Word of God in the words of the Bible, but that God has words for us in our creation also. We are constantly being surprised.

Bishop Tom Butler
West Yorkshire

Religion and the Gulf Wars

Probably no event, or series of events has been more divisive during the last two decades than the Gulf wars. They have divided opinion within Britain and Europe and have had a detrimental effect on relationships between Muslim and Western countries. With emotions beginning to calm with a new generation of political leaders, now is perhaps a good time to seek to examine events and decisions using the time honoured Christian criteria for the 'just war', which since the time of Thomas Aquinas in the thirteenth century has provided rulers and ruled with a benchmark to consider whether it is right to go to war or engage in a rebellion against civic powers. It might be thought that the concept of the just war is rather dated when considering modern warfare and weaponry, but it is on the syllabus of military academies as well as theological colleges and, as we shall see, gives us a very helpful perspective in judging the wisdom or otherwise of engaging in the Gulf wars.

The criteria for the just war are well known. Because Christian teaching honours both human life and a society working for the common good, it sees the killing of individuals as a serious sin which we should strive to avoid. Because of this many Christians, amongst others, refuse to take up arms whatever the cause. This has not been the mainline position of the Church, however. Rather taking up arms in self defence or in the face of an oppressive regime has been seen as a legitimate last resort with several provisos.

First of all, other methods of ending the dispute must have been attempted and failed. Secondly, there must be legitimate and lawful authority for going to war. Thirdly, the war must be fought with the right intention; material gain for example, is not a just purpose. Fourthly, because all war causes suffering, there must be a reasonable belief that the war will have a successful outcome; if there is doubt here, it might be better to live with some injustice and oppression, rather than cause great suffering to no human benefit.

If it is judged that these conditions have been met and that going to war is legitimate then other criteria kick in concerning the conduct of the war. As far as is possible war must only be fought against enemy soldiers and civilian casualties should be avoided. Once enemy soldiers have surrendered and have been disarmed they must be treated with respect. With modern weaponry getting more and more powerful it might be thought that the avoidance of civilian casualties is a vain hope, but it has been claimed that the development of 'smart' weapons gives military commanders more control over the destruction they cause. In any event, another criteria within war is that the force used must be proportionate to the wrong that has been done and the possible good that can come out of the war; a wasteland of burning oil fields, for example would be to nobody's benefit. In general, the force and weaponry used should be the minimum necessary to achieve the desired outcome.

There are further criteria for a just cause to end the war. The stated desired aim should have been met and terms of surrender negotiated: also, even a war having a just cause can be ended if it is clear that victory cannot be achieved. Peace terms must be negotiated and agreed between legitimate authorities and should be proportionate to the original reason for going to war and should not be the cause of such grievance, resentment or hardship such as to plant the seeds of a further future conflict. There must be no revenge taken and any punishment should be limited to those who were directly responsible for the conflict.

Unpacking the events of the Gulf wars within the perspective of these criteria is instructive, not least because the messy outcome of the First Gulf War simmered throughout the next decade and overlapped with the given causes of a Second Gulf War. Eight 'Thought' scripts are included here from different times during these disputes and illustrate how, at the time, I was trying to interpret day-by-day events.

The first 'Thought' comes from January 1991, six months after Iraq's invasion of Kuwait. Of course this invasion came out of turmoil in the region in earlier years. Almost one million people died in the Iraq–Iran war from 1980 until 1989. In 1981 Israel had bombed the Iraqi nuclear plant near Baghdad. In 1987 there had been reports of Iraqi chemical attacks on Kurdish villages, and soil samples confirmed the use of mustard gas and the nerve agent Tabun.

The immediate response to the Iraqi invasion of Kuwait in August 1990 was a series of UN resolutions calling for Iraqi withdrawal, stating that the annexation had no legal validity, demanding the release of foreign nationals that Iraq was detaining and, in some cases, using as hostages in Iraq and Kuwait. At the same time the UN called for economic sanctions against Iraq. In September 1990 Iraq called for the overthrow of leaders in Saudi Arabia and Egypt, and there was US military build-up in Saudi Arabia. On 9 September there was a joint US–Soviet statement affirming the principle that 'we must demonstrate beyond any doubt that aggression cannot and will not pay'. Finally, at the end of November, UN resolution 678 authorized the use of 'all means necessary' after 15 January 1991 to enforce previous UN resolutions, including that requiring Iraqi withdrawal from Kuwait.

With all of this it would seem that all the just conditions for going to war had been met. The invasion of Kuwait by Iraq had been ruled by the UN to be illegal and illegitimate. Other diplomatic and economic pressure had been attempted and force would be being used as a necessary last resort, with legitimate authority and with the aim of forcing Iraq to withdraw from Kuwait. This thinking was behind the 'Thought' script, delivered on 2 January 1991, which anticipated the use of allied force, yet expressed the hope that 'now the world community, having shown its willingness to shoulder bravely its load of care, find a way of ensuring freedom and justice without precipitating itself into the horror of war'. This hope was not realized and 'Operation Desert Storm' began with an Apache helicopter strike on 17 January 1991.

ZULU, 2 JANUARY 1991

The film Zulu was shown on television again just after Christmas. It tells the story of an engineering officer who, with his platoon of soldiers, was sent way out into the bush to build a bridge across a river in South Africa. Whilst there they were attacked out of the blue by a large force of Zulu warriors. An unexpected load had to be shouldered by the officer, a load of care – the defence of his men.

The load of care soon grew because, as senior officer, the defence of the whole area became his responsibility. Before long the war started in earnest. The Zulus attacked in wave after wave. Many of the British soldiers were killed. Others fought on bravely yet, finally, it seemed that all was lost. The Zulus grouped for a last attack. But then, astonishingly, instead of pressing home their advantage, they formed up and saluted the British soldiers for their bravery and they then withdrew, leaving the commanding officer smiling with relief and saying, 'After all, I only came here to build a bridge.'

The load of care is often so. It comes out of the blue. It expands, yet those shouldering it bravely can win respect and even honour. Christians at least shouldn't be surprised by this, for Jesus of Nazareth bore an ever expanding load of care. First as teacher and healer in the hills of Galilee; then as prophet in Jerusalem; finally as crucified saviour of the world. And it was an unknown Roman soldier who, witnessing Jesus's courage on the cross, spoke wiser words than he knew, words of honour and respect: 'Behold the man.'

The hero of our film went out to build a bridge, yet he found himself, with his comrades, caught up in something quite different – a fearsome war. Our thoughts at the present time go out to those of all nations who fear that they too might be caught up in the midst of a brutal war. Perhaps they joined the army, British, American, Syrian, Egyptian, to see the world, or learn a skill, or perhaps they were bored, or wanted to do their bit for their country. Whatever they thought they were doing, now they're in the desert sand protecting freedom, or oil, or the world economy, facing a war that might seem to be the least of several evils, but is no less terrifying for that. The load of care has expanded and they and we are stuck with it.

In the film it took the slaughter of a large proportion of the young Zulu and British warriors before mutual respect brought the battle to an end. It's sad that such mutual respect and honour can't more often be found before a war rather that after it, for sometimes the negotiations of the thoughtful can be just as heroic as the dogmatic certainties of the belligerent. In the Gulf, Iraqi expansionism has been halted by a swift and steadfast use of military force. Might now the world community, having shown its willingness to shoulder bravely its load of care, find a way of ensuring freedom and justice without precipitating itself into the horror of war? If so, the world might know a happier New Year. [The defence of Rorke's Drift on 22–23 January 1879 – the event portrayed in the film *Zulu* – occurred after a Zulu army had wiped out a British column of more than 1,300 men at the Battle of Isandlwana earlier on 22 January.]

Within six weeks the fighting was over but not before Scud missiles had hit Israel. The aftermath of the war was to prove to be rather more controversial than the war itself. The UN resolution 687 in April established the peace terms, including the return of Kuwaiti property, economic sanctions and Iraqi disarmament. Iraq was to provide a list of all weapons of mass destruction (WMD) in its possession. United Nations Special Commission (UNSCOM) inspectors were to ascertain that the arms had been surrendered. Here lay the seeds of a future war, for there never was agreement that Iraq had declared or surrendered all of its WMD.

President George Bush (Sr) was criticized by some for halting the war as soon as its objectives had been achieved, the expulsion of Iraqi forces from Kuwait. Many felt that the allied forces should have gone on and finished the job with the expulsion of Saddam Hussein from power. In terms of just war criteria, however, President Bush's action was quite correct, for the UN had not given authority for regime change. This would clearly have been seen as an illegal action with little support from neighbouring countries.

However, another consequence of careless planning following the ceasefire could be criticized. At the end of March, with US encouragement, the Shia in the south of Iraq and the Kurds in the north rebelled against the Saddam Hussein regime. The Iraqi army and air force had not been disarmed and within a month the rebels were crushed with approximately one and a half million Kurds fleeing into neighbouring countries.

The 'Thought' of 9 April 1991 speaks to this peace plan that has gone astray. It compares the Shiite and Kurdish rebels to a class's pet snake. During the half-term holidays the teacher left a live rat for food in the snake's tank. Unfortunately for the snake, the cleaner turned off the heat and the snake went into a deep sleep. When the class returned that snake had not eaten the rat, the rat had eaten the snake. Following the war, Saddam Hussein, the rat, was very much alive and dangerous. As events in Iraq unfolded, the just war criteria of giving just as much attention to building a just peace as to planning and waging a just war are well illustrated, and because, with the best will in the world, there will be unforeseen consequences, those waging war must always be ready to generously contribute to the care of the casualties, not only of the war, but of the peace.

SADDAM HUSSEIN AND THE SNAKE, 9 APRIL 1991

A year or so ago I read about a teacher who'd attempted to keep her class's pet snake well fed during the school half-term holiday by leaving a small live rat in the tank with the snake when the class went home. Unfortunately for the snake the school cleaner switched off the tank's heating system along with the school room lights when she went home. As the tank cooled, the snake went into a deep sleep and when the teacher returned from her holidays she was horrified to find that the snake had not eaten the rat, but the rat had eaten the snake.

Something similar seems to be happening in the Middle East. The plan of the allies following the war with Iraq surely was to leave behind a snake of rebellion which would eat the rat-like Saddam Hussein. Unfortunately for the Shiite and Kurdish rebels, it seems that the snake of rebellion has not eaten the rat, but the rat, still armed to the teeth, is busily eating the snake.

A military friend of mine told me before the war started that a plan of war rarely survives the outbreak of hostilities – the unexpected invariably happens. Now it seems that the plan of peace has not survived the ceasefire – the unexpected has happened. It is ever so. To paraphrase Robert Burns – the best laid schemes of mice and men tend to go astray.

It's just because human plans do tend to go astray that protection, compassion and charitable-giving feature high in the demands of any world religion – for the battered victims of human and natural disasters are ever with us. The story is told of a rich man who, when he went for prayer, was led by his servants along a route which avoided meeting with any people begging for food or healing, because it was believed that to hear the cries of suffering people and not respond to their needs turned the heart to stone. And so it does, but the answer is not to protect our humanity by avoiding the cries of the needy; the answer is to protect their humanity by mobilizing our hearts and minds to better their situation.

St Paul, even whilst he was spreading Christianity amongst the fringe people of the cities of the Mediterranean world, at the same time was collecting money from them, to ease the suffering of those in Jerusalem who'd been dispossessed due to war or religious faith.

Avoiding the cries of the needy then is not a luxury open to people of faith – and it is certainly not a luxury open in this situation to those of us from the nations which made up the allied armies. The casualties of peace are an unforeseen consequence of a war undertaken in good faith and a peace plan which has gone badly astray. As a nation we were prepared to dig deeply into our pockets to fund the war, we had now better dig even more deeply in it if the casualties are to be tended, and a true peace is ever to be found.

For the next three years occasional skirmishes occurred until in November 1994 the Iraq National Assembly officially acknowledged Kuwaiti sovereignty with Saddam Hussein ratifying the decision the same day.

It was in this year that David Steele, now Lord Steele, and I paid a humanitarian fact-finding visit to Iraq to seek to judge how sanctions were effecting the life of Iraq's schools and hospitals. With air links cut, we travelled across the desert in an ancient taxi from Amman. We were met in Bagdad by the Baath party official who was to be our constant and attentive 'minder'. This was useful in arranging visits to institutions and government ministers, but it was quite obvious that nobody was going to be at all critical in his presence. At 2 p.m. each afternoon, however, he delivered us to our rooms for an afternoon nap, collecting us later at 4.30 pm. We used the afternoon not in sleep but in slipping out to meet NGOs and Church members who fed us with useful and perceptive questions to ask of ministers the following day. I mention this visit in my 'Thought' of 4 February 1998 when military action was once more being discussed.

IRAQ, 4 FEBRUARY 1998

There's a flawed logic which goes like this. The situation is terrible. Something must be done. This is something. Therefore we must do it. I fear that this kind of logic might lead to premature air strikes on Iraq.

The situation is terrible. Saddam Hussein is a danger to his own people and neighbouring countries. Something must be done. But is an air strike the 'something'? In 1994, three years after the end of the Gulf War, Sir David Steele and I went on a humanitarian fact-finding visit to Iraq. We had an official programme of visits to hospitals and clinics, but we were also quite skilful at slipping away to pay private visits to ordinary Church people. Speaking for myself, I wasn't too surprised by the atmosphere of fear – but you could cut it with a knife, I was surprised and disturbed by the extent of child malnutrition and disease – sanctions were biting deeply even then, and I was astonished at the fury and the blame which ordinary folk directed, not at their own government and its leader, but at the United States and Britain because of the air strikes and sanctions. You can put it down to propaganda or to national patriotism, but there was no doubting its reality and I doubt whether much has changed in four years.

Jesus Christ, who could be remarkably hard headed at times, once said, that no king goes to war without very carefully counting the cost of the enterprise and the chances of success. Later this became one of the basic principles behind the categories of a just war. War inevitably causes damage and death to the innocent, so you should weigh up the outcome of the war very carefully before embarking upon it, and in particular you should weigh up whether the likely gains will be worth the innocent suffering which will be caused.

When Sir David and I were leaving Iraq we were parked at the border post in a VIP lounge. We were joined by an Iraqi minister entering his country from Jordan. He engaged us in a civilized conversation and then because it was midday Friday went to say his prayers kneeling on the corner of the carpet. He returned to continue the conversation and as he did so he casually took out a revolver and started loading it. That brief encounter spoke volumes to me. Iraq is a country of deep civilization, piety, and violence. Dealing with such a country requires patience, firmness, subtlety and persistence – I doubt whether the big bang of air strikes will be as effective, but I'm glad that it is politicians not Churchmen who at the end of the day have to take the decisions. They have my sympathy and my prayers.

The visit to Bagdad had been wearing and depressing. People were obviously living in a state of fear under a totalitarian regime and children were suffering from malnutrition. We reported this to the authorities back in the UK and I was relieved when some months later in April 1995 UN Resolution 986 established the 'Oil for Food' programme.

Within four months two of Saddam Hussein's sons-in-law defected to Jordan, taking with them crates of documents revealing past concealment of WMD capacities and the fact that Iraq had begun an unsuccessful crash programme to develop a nuclear bomb. All of this, of course, lay at the heart of the UN's determination to seek out WDM material and the utter refusal of the British and American governments to believe that Iraq had done so. It seems that Saddam Hussein was deliberately feeding this perception, a kind of double bluff which was later to have tragic consequences. I had no hint of this, of course, but as UNSCOM inspectors were frustrated in their work and were finally asked to leave Iraq in November 1997, the talk of further air strikes was in the air and I felt we were leaving the aftermath of one Gulf War and were entering the territory of preparing for another. In my February 1998 Thought, taking the parable of Jesus Christ about a king weighing up his chances of success before going to war (a just war criteria), and calling upon the experience of our 1994 visit, I pointed out that Iraq is a country of deep civilization, piety and violence. Dealing with such a country requires patience, firmness, subtlety and persistence rather than the big bang of air strikes.

In December 1998 the big bang of the air strikes came, however. After UN staff had been evacuated from Baghdad, the US and the UK launched a bombing campaign, 'Operation Desert Fox', aiming to destroy Iraq's nuclear, chemical and biological weapons programme. In the following year the UN passed a resolution creating a new Verification and Inspection Commission. Iraq rejected the resolution. Britain and the US carried out further bombing raids to try to disable Iraq's air defence network. The raids had little international support. Then came 9/11 2001 and the terror attack on the World Trade Center in New York.

Immediately, President Bush (Jr) declared a 'War on Terror', targeting Iraq, amongst others, in an 'Axis of Evil', with speculation growing that Iraq might have had a hand in training the hijackers. I presented three 'Thoughts' in the month following 9/11. I will refer to the first in the following chapter on 'Terrorism'! The third was given on 23 September 2001 by which time British and US jets had bombed surface-to-air missile batteries in southern Iraq. In my 'Thought' I pointed out once more that Christian ethics teaches that military action must always be a last resort. I flagged up that it seemed that we had passed the point of no return and such action was inevitable and so I moved onto the criteria for the conduct of a just war – that such action had to be proportionate. Of course we were all still stunned by the 9/11 attack and the murder of around 3,000 unsuspecting people and so it was not surprising if punishment and retribution might have been in the forefront of those planning the strategy for war. My 'Thought' insisted that discrimination must drive this war, and the aim should not only be to cut down terrorism root and branch but not to pollute the soil of a future peace. 'Unless we tend the soil of tomorrow, we can't truly win the war of today.'

IT'S WAR, 24 SEPTEMBER 2001

So it really is war and we have to add images of exploding missiles to the image of the exploding planes and falling towers which are still seared into our minds. There may well be feelings of excitement and patriotism, but these are mixed with feelings of anxiety and dread and a sense that it's always easier to get into a war than to get out, particularly when the enemy are fanatics driven by ideology.

And this is a Monday morning and yesterday as usual I was out preaching the Christian gospel in church and chapel. So how am I to relate that to what's going on in the world today?

Military action must be a last resort – that's what the Christian ethical theory says – when all other ways of persuasion and negotiation have failed. Well, rightly or wrongly we seem to be past the point of no return and military action has started. So next – any such action must be proportionate. Well, what action is proportionate to respond to the murder of around 3,000 unsuspecting people going about their business on a sunny September morning? And it's not just they who have to be borne in mind. What if the worst nightmares are true and on the terrorists' future agenda are plans for germ warfare or briefcase nuclear weapons. Our cities would become cemeteries. The purpose of this war might in some minds be a question of punishment or retribution but it's the prevention of future crimes which should be in the forefront of the minds of those planning the strategies.

So above all, discrimination must drive this war, and not just discrim-ination between the guilty and the innocent, and God knows too many innocent victims in tower block and refugee camp have already suffered. This must be a war which seeks and eliminates the terrorists without entering into confrontation with whole states. The action must be akin to targeting cancerous cells rather than cutting off whole limbs.

And Christian ethical theory won't let us stop there. Yes, it talks about retribution and punishment and the prevention of future crimes but it also points to justice and reconciliation and healing. And when this messy war is finally over we have all got to continue to share this one precious and vulnerable planet. The aim may be to cut down terrorism root and branch but by doing that we must not so pollute the soil that nothing good can grow. The present terrorists have grown in the polluted injustice. Perhaps the gospel message is that unless we tend the soil of tomorrow we can't truly win the war of today.

In the event, the war was a long time in coming. Throughout 2002 when no doubt military preparations were being made on all sides there were two other fields of activity. Negotiations continued seeking the agreement of Iraq to the inspectors return and this was finally given in August 2002. In September 2002 US President George W. Bush told sceptical world leaders at a UN General Assembly session to confront the 'grave and gathering danger' of Iraq or stand aside as the US acts.

The other activity concerned the British government's determination to provide a legal justification for a new Gulf War. Legality had not been a problem with the First Gulf War, for Iraq had clearly invaded an independent neighbouring state and the allies had both UN resolutions and support in taking action to repel them.

The situation was different this time. There was no clear evidence that Iraq had been involved with the 9/11 attacks and it was not indicating military action against any neighbour. Saddam Hussein's regime might be oppressive and brutal (in my personal experience it was both), but this does not give legality to a third nation to take military action seeking regime change. It must be said, however, that the UK had taken such action earlier in both Bosnia and Sierra Leone with generally beneficial results in both countries. Nevertheless, Tony Blair realized that with Iraq there must be clearer evidence that the UK and other powers were directly threatened if agreement was to be given by Parliament and the UN to military action, and without such agreements the action would be illegal.

In September 2002 Tony Blair released a dossier coming from intelligence sources and showing that Iraq had significant WMD capabilities. The UN inspectors returned to Iraq in November 2002, backed by a UN resolution which threatened serious consequences if Iraq was in 'material breach' of its terms.

In October 2002 the Church of England House of Bishops made a submission to the Foreign Affairs Subcommittee setting a high threshold for any Iraq War and followed the submission with a statement in January 2003 asserting that the case for war has yet to be made. I, with the Roman Catholic Bishop of Leeds, was deputed to meet with the Foreign Secretary, Jack Straw, to draw our concerns to his attention. Speaking with him I had no doubt that he believed that war was inevitable. I asked him whether he was absolutely sure that military action would uncover WMD. He said that he was. I asked his opinion as to the best and worst outcome of such military action. He said that the best outcome would be for the Iraqi armed forces to put up little or no resistance, for the allied forces to be received as liberators, with a democratic government being swiftly established. The worst outcome, we speculated, would be a fierce fight for Baghdad followed by years of guerrilla warfare, with neighbouring states joining in the hostilities. On the basis of this meeting it does not seem, therefore, that no thought had been given to life after the invasion, but sadly, in the event the outcome has proved nearer the worst hope than the best.

The British government continued to encourage the US to seek a further mandate from the UN authorizing the coming war. In March the Chief Weapons Inspector, Hans Blix, reported to the UN Security

Council that Iraq had accelerated its cooperation but said that the inspectors needed more time to verify Iraq's compliance. The US and UK called for a second resolution authorizing a war against Iraq but this met with stiff opposition from France, Russia, Germany and Arab countries.

The British Attorney General, having met further with President Bush's legal advisers, reported to the Prime Minister that he was satisfied of the legality of the planned military action on the basis of the previous UN resolutions. It should be said that this was a very important matter, not only for getting the agreement of the British Parliament for the coming war, but also because without such legal cover it is not certain that the military Chiefs of Staff would have been prepared to lead British troops into a war. They were wary of a conflict that might have a dubious legal status. This, of course, has remained an issue much discussed and disputed and it might be added that it is not always realized that an action might be strictly legal without it being clearly legitimate.

War began on 19 March 2003 with US forces invading southern Iraq and at first meeting light resistance. The resistance increased, however, until by 4 April the troops had reached the 'Red Line' around Baghdad. I presented a 'Thought' on that day which I called 'Crossing the Rubicon'. It is instructive because it is a reminder that by that stage we still did not know whether the Iraqis had stocks of chemical weapons. I indicated that I hoped that the intelligence had been wrong and that there were no such deployable weaponry, for if it existed, it would surely be used that day and would risk the lives of the US troops. My earlier meeting with the Foreign Secretary must also have been in my mind as I flagged up the risk of getting bogged down in urban guerrilla fighting.

CROSSING THE RUBICON, 3 APRIL 2003

When Julius Caesar in 49 BC with his army crossed the River Rubicon, he crossed from Gaul into Italy, he passed out of the limits of the province for which he had responsibility and became an invader of the homeland, and thus the war with Pompey and the Senate became inevitable.

United States soldiers during the past 24 hours have equally crossed a significant frontier – the so-called red line around Baghdad; there's fighting at the airport and the battle for the capital has begun. The nature of that battle is still uncertain. The best prognosis would see the Republican Guard and the Baath party government and its supporters rapidly collapsing and the people of Iraq grasping the opportunity for building a better future for themselves and the region. The worst prognosis sees the American and British army bogged down in urban guerrilla fighting – Northern Ireland or the Lebanon at its worst.

But that's for the future. For now, crossing the Rubicon, the red line around Baghdad, has been marked in a significant way by US troops and the reporters accompanying them. They've put on chemical protective suits underneath their body armour. Now if Saddam Hussein has been telling the truth, this protection is unnecessary because Iraq doesn't possess chemical weapons. But if he's been lying then now will be the time when any such weapons will be used. This would have the dubious comfort of justifying one of the stated reasons for the war – to destroy weapons of mass destruction – but at the cost of the risk of the lives of US troops. So they put on extra protection under the armour.

The words of St Paul in his Epistle to the Ephesians suddenly seem remarkably modern. 'Put on the whole armour of God that ye may be able to stand against the wiles of the devil. Take unto you the whole armour of God that ye may be able to withstand in the evil day, and having done all, to stand.'

The armour which the soldiers are putting on today is all too real and physical. Paul was referring to armour of a different reality – the reality of truth, righteousness, peace, faith, salvation. This is the armour which is all too relevant to us as we go into the skirmishes of everyday living. And it could be that in the midst of those skirmishes today a significant moral or spiritual frontier is crossed. The Rubicon between Gaul and Italy was no great river; it really was no more than a stream – trivial. Yet it marked the point of no return. Perhaps whilst being concerned about the world at war we should also be alert to such moral frontiers in our own lives and keep our spiritual armour in good repair.

The early signs were hopeful, however. Within a month Saddam Hussein had fled and I presented a 'Thought' on 8 April linking the image of his statue being pulled to the ground in Basra with the meeting of the Archbishop of Canterbury that day with Christian and Muslim scholars in Qatar. I indicated that the war was not basically a war between religions. Sadly, it has been difficult to convince young Muslims of this, which has helped to make the response of terrorism more intense as we shall see in the next chapter. The reputation of the Coalition forces was damaged further by highly publicized mistreatment of Iraqi prisoners by some US and British troops. All were brought before courts and punished, but the damage had already been done. In particular, the pictures of maltreatment of prisoners amounting to torture by US guards in the Abu Graib prison were widely circulated, whilst as recently as March 2011 a US soldier in Iraq admitted being part of a group who were killing Iraqi civilians 'for sport'. St Thomas Aquinas in his reflections upon a just war wrote, 'Action follows Being'. The question is not solely 'Have we got the right rules and are our forces following them?' but also, 'Are our forces made up of individuals who are the right people with sound moral instincts?' This is a far more difficult thing to judge, but when soldiers are faced with taking instant decisions in the heat of battle their instincts govern their behaviour.

STALIN'S EAR, 8 APRIL 2003

The image of the gigantic statue of Saddam Hussein being pulled to the ground in Bazra reminded me of a report I heard from a different country. The reporter was talking of life today in a country previously behind the Iron Curtain. There used to be an enormous statue of Stalin standing in one of the city's parks. Then the miracle happened. Communism was overthrown, and the first thing that the people had done was to pull down the statue and it had been broken into bits. One piece, however, had remained in the park. It was the ear of the statue, and such had been the statue's great size, that the ear is now being used as a small swimming pool. The ear of the statue of fear is now the vessel of fun and laughter.

Human beings have a great capacity for reinventing themselves and their world and recovering from the most severe setbacks. It's too early to see what the future might hold for the people of Iraq. At present we see a mix of fear, patriotism, courage, relief, pride and fury. The toppling of the statues of Saddam Hussein may be symbolic to them both of the end of his regime and of invasion by foreign forces. It's a time of turmoil and trauma, but new life will come and the parks and cafés of Baghdad will echo with laughter once more.

The focus of our thoughts at the moment is the present war but there are other signs today of that promise of new life. Christian and Muslim scholars including the Archbishop of Canterbury are meeting in Qatar to discuss – not the war, for this is not basically a war between religions – no, they are meeting to discuss the interpretation of holy scripture, discussions which will continue long into the future, and hopefully be part of the glue which will hold the worlds of Islam and the West together in the decades ahead. President Bush and our Prime Minister meet in Belfast, again not only to discuss Iraq but to meet with the political leaders who, if they have the will, can help create a more peaceful and prosperous future for the peoples of Northern Ireland, a future which was beyond anyone's dreams even a decade ago.

Shelley in his poem 'Ozymandias' recorded the words engraved on the broken statue in the desert sands, 'My name is Ozymandias, King of Kings; Look on my works, ye Mighty, and despair.' But the new life in Stalin's ear can give us hope not despair. Easter is two weeks away. Like the ear on Stalin's statue, nothing could have been more dead and lifeless than the tomb holding the crucified body of Jesus Christ yet God smashed the tomb to smithereens and the risen Jesus brought new and joyful life to the world, a world expecting nothing of the sort.

President Bush declared an end to the war, barely six weeks after it had begun, on 1 May 2003 but although the war might have ended the aftermath was difficult and dangerous. Peacemaking and peacekeeping were to prove to be more difficult than waging the war itself, particularly as the US administration were determined that no one serving the previous Baath regime was to keep their post. As this included virtually every member of the armed forces and police together with every civil servant the structures of civil society swiftly collapsed. Within two months Saddam Hussein had been captured and his two sons killed in a shoot out with US troops, but the civil terror had also begun.

A foretaste was the bombing of a UN compound killing 20. Then an explosion near the Najaf Mosque killed over 90 including the Shiite leader Ayatollah Mohammed Bakir al-Hakim. The killings continued into 2004 with a further 270 Shi'a worshippers killed during Ashura holy day rites in a suicide bombing, and as the date on which sovereignty was to be handed over, 28 June approached, coordinated terror attacks became an almost daily occurrence. I presented a 'Thought' on 29 June 2004 pointing to these self-inflicted wounds as a form of civic self-abuse. I had visited Babylon during my 1994 humanitarian visit. Then images of Saddam Hussein stood alongside those of Nebuchadnezzar. I pointed to the prophet Jeremiah's advice to the people of Israel in exile in Babylon: 'It is in everyone's interest to help rebuild the city.' I suggested that in these post-war days the time of weeping should be over and the time of rebuilding begun.

IRAQ AND URBAN FOXES 29 JUNE 2004

I used to have a large golden retriever dog of which I was very fond. He came in one afternoon dripping with blood from a deep gash in his ear. He had obviously come off worst in a skirmish with the urban foxes who inhabit my garden. I took him to the vet; told her of the fight with the foxes and was then rather surprised when she started poking about inside the other ear. 'You're looking at the wrong ear,' I said, 'No I'm not,' she replied. 'This has nothing to do with foxes. Your dog has an infection in both ears, and he's wounded himself by scratching at it with his back paw.'

The people of Iraq, of course, are infinitely more precious than any dog but they too have known many wounds in past years. But yesterday marked a significant change in nation building, or so we hope. The urban foxes are back in their barrack, but the wounds for some months now have not been caused by them. No, they've been self-inflicted acts of terror coming from a complex infection of secular fascist forces from the old Baath party and religious zealots from outside, only too happy to die for their faith.

Will this civil self-abuse continue now that the provisional Iraqi government is in office if not yet in real power? We shall soon see whether the glorious or the ghastly side of Iraqi life prevails, and as always it is the ordinary people of Iraq who will bear the wounds, if wounds there continue to be.

A word from faith history might encourage them. Some two and a half thousand years ago the great king Nebuchadnezzar sacked Jerusalem and took most of its population into exile in Babylon – modern Iraq. When the exiles saw the huge monuments and palaces they were in trauma. Their feelings are recorded in an Old Testament psalm: 'By the river of Babylon I sat down and wept when I remembered you O Zion.' They alternated periods of deep despair with wish dreaming that they would soon be home.

The prophet Jeremiah pulled them back to reality. He wrote, 'Build houses and settle down. Plant gardens and eat what they produce. Seek the peace and prosperity of the city. Pray to the Lord for it, because if it prospers, you too will prosper. Do not let false prophets deceive you. Don't listen to the dreams you encourage them to have.' The Lord says, 'I know the plans I have to prosper you. Plans to give you a hope and a future.'

May the people of Iraq have a hope and a future and may we find the way to encourage and strengthen them whilst we seek to heal the wounds which the war has caused not only with our relationships with nations in

the Arab world but also with communities of faith in Britain. The time
of weeping is over. The time of rebuilding has begun.

The civil disorder and sectarian violence was to continue, however, even
with the withdrawal of US troops from front-line duties. Polling day in
the US was 7 November 2006, and Saddam Hussein was standing in
the dock in Iraq. My 'Thought' of that day returned to Aquinas's just
war criteria. In particular, it reminded listeners of one particular factor:
because all war involves disorder, it is sometimes better to endure a degree
of injustice and oppression rather than face the chaos of war because a
disordered society bears most heavily on the weak and powerless. It
might be fruitless, I suggested, to ask whether, facing today's anarchy,
were the Iraqi people not better served by Saddam's ordered security
where the water and electricity flowed and the schools and hospitals
were open and every child had a daily food ration. I suppose the major
gain is that, in the days of Saddam Hussein, nobody would have dared to
ask such a question. With the disappearance of the war leaders from the
stage perhaps the emotional and tribal divisions of Iraq will mollify and
the difficult business of nation building can seriously begin.

SADDAM AND THE US ELECTION, 7 NOVEMBER 2006

Seeing Saddam Hussein in the dock after three years in captivity, seeking
to shout down the judge pronouncing sentence was a reminder of the
sheer brutal power of the man. I paid a humanitarian visit to Iraq after
the First Gulf War and was depressed by the climate of fear stemming
from that cruel powerful man that seemed to penetrate every element of
Iraqi life. And yet water and electricity flowed, schools and shops were
open, people got on with their everyday life by keeping their heads down
and not getting involved in the oppression all around.

Now, Saddam has gone – almost – sectarian death squads roam the
streets of Baghdad, basic utilities are problematic, and nobody is safe.

Saint Thomas Aquinas eight centuries ago in seeking to codify the
ethical conditions which would support a just war or a just rebellion

included the factor that, because all war involves disorder, it is better sometimes, rather than go to war, to put up with a degree of injustice and even oppression, because a disordered society bears mostly heavily on the weak and powerless. It's fruitless to ask ourselves whether the Iraqi people were better off under Saddam's brutal rule than they are under today's anarchy for there is no going back. But as America goes to the polls today there will be many who will be asking themselves whether the war was worth it, and what the future holds for Iraq and America.

The English historian Arnold Toynbee once wrote that America is like a large friendly dog in a very small room. Every time it wags its tail, it knocks over a chair. I hope that the shifting furniture after today's elections gives less influence to what are called Christian end-timers – those apocalyptic dreamers who believe that history is about to be wound up and are quite prepared for the American government to give God a hand in winding it up more quickly. One of their leaders recently claimed that the Bush Sr administration would sometimes take their calls, whilst the advisers of this administration call them and ask, 'What's your take on this issue?' Hopefully now, the telephone will be taken off the hook once more, for this is no time for apocalyptic dreaming; it's a time for thoughtful, careful, patient, painful nation building.

It's instructive to realize that within two years, the three political leaders most closely involved with the war in Iraq – Saddam Hussein, President Bush, and Tony Blair – like it or not, will all in different ways have left the world stage. Responsibility for the future of their countries will have passed into other hands. I hope they'll bear in mind that all significant moral decisions involve the questions, 'Who at the end of the day gets hurt and how can that hurt be minimized?'

The execution of Saddam Hussein did not, of course, end the Iraq story. Even after the withdrawal of British troops from Basra, and with a type of elected Iraqi government in place, atrocities, including suicide bombings, continued, now often more sectarian in nature.

The arguments concerning the legality of the war continued with the Chilcot Inquiry reporting in 2011. Certainly involvement in Iraq and Afghanistan colours the reputation the US and Britain has throughout the Arab world and is a factor in President Obama's reluctance for US troops to take a leadership position in the actions against the Gaddafi regime in Libya in 2011. Above all, of course, the repercussions of the war in Iraq has affected community cohesion in Britain. We will turn to this in the following chapter.

2

Religion and Terrorism

The 'War on Terror' unleashed by President Bush as a response to the 9/11 atrocity has not, of course, been confined to Iraq, Afghanistan, Israel and Palestine. Terrorism is to now to be found on the streets of London and other Western cities, although in the case of London it is worth reminding ourselves that we have seen the weapon of terror being used for religious reasons on our streets before. In a script of 13 July 1989 I remarked on a terror threat to Billy Graham in his final meeting in Wembley Stadium and referred to a sad parable of Protestant and Roman Catholic children in Northern Ireland returning on a bus from an enjoyable holiday together, and then stoning the bus the moment they stepped down into their sectarian home setting. Of course, this 'Thought' might also be seen as a parable of hope, because it reminds us of the progress which has been made in 20 years in breaking down sectarian barriers.

STONED THE BUS, 13 JULY 1989

I attended Billy Graham's final meeting at Wembley Stadium last Saturday. In addition to a dramatic thunderstorm Billy Graham had to contend with death threats, apparently made because his supporting singer happened to be an Irish Roman Catholic. How sad.

A few years ago one of my students spent her vacation helping to run a children's holiday club in Northern Ireland. The children came from both sides of the religious divide and thoroughly enjoyed their fortnight's holiday away together, and the helpers, though exhausted by it all, were congratulating themselves that they'd made a real contribution to breaking down sectarianism and strife.

They were driving the children home in a bus which stopped in one of the areas of town, I really can't remember whether it was Protestant or Catholic. The bus stopped to let one of the groups of children out. The children said their goodbyes and stepped down from the bus. Then as it drove away, these same children joined in with the other local kids in stoning the bus.

That's rather a depressing parable of the difficulties which lie before those who seek to break down the barriers between religious opponents. Hostilities which have festered over the centuries are not easily healed in a few weeks, and folk who live in enclosed communities where everybody agrees to agree soon revert to type when they come under stress.

I'm with the Archbishop of Canterbury when he questions the kind of religious fundamentalism which degenerates into fanaticism, for there's all the difference in the world between a faith of mellow certainty, and the hard dogmatism which seems to outsiders to be sterile and unattractive. The difference is that a person may die for a living faith, but will kill for a dying dogma.

Narrow fundamentalism just will not work. It will work in the short term, possibly, if people are pounded hard enough, and they're feeling wobbly under the pressures of modern life, but in the long term it can't work, because it shuts out too much of what we known to be true about the world.

But let's not be too gloomy. There are chinks of light. Rangers, traditionally top, or thereabouts, of the Scottish football league, and also traditionally a centre of Protestantism, has signed its first Catholic player, Mo Johnston, for £1.5 million. The cynics are saying that this merely demonstrates that Rangers desperately need a brilliant striker. But I see it as a sign of increasing tolerance in our society. There's a New York church which sets a great example of this kind of tolerance. It has a notice outside which reads, 'All people are welcome here, whatever their age, sex, denomination, or the number of times that they've been born again.'

In the 'Thought' I refer to religious fundamentalism which can degen-
erate into fanaticism for which people will not only die, but kill. There
seem to be three ingredients feeding modern movements of terror.
Firstly, there is this progression from a traditional faith to a more fundamentalist form and then to its violent expression. Secondly, there is a
political ingredient where terror is seen as the sole weapon for a people's
perceived oppression. Thirdly, there is often something going on in the
personal life of the recruit to terrorism.

Whilst the Northern Irish situation reminds us that modern terrorism
is not confined to Islam it is salutary also to remind ourselves that not
every Roman Catholic in Ireland became a member of the IRA and not
every member of the IRA pursued a path of terror in response to political
pressures. Equally we must distinguish between 'Islam' – a whole system
of beliefs of 1.3 billion Muslims around the world – and 'Islamism' – a
radical form of Islamic fundamentalism with a political as well as a
religious dimension – and 'Islamist terrorism' – terrorism carried out by
Muslims in the name of Islam. It would be a grave error to believe that
terrorism is a natural expression of Islamic beliefs, anymore than it is a
natural expression of Roman Catholic or Protestant Christian beliefs.

The political ingredient in the Islamic terrorism mix well predates
9/11 or even the Iraq wars; it has festered in Palestinian consciousness
since Palestinians were deprived of lands and property by the creation
of the state of Israel and this itself was preceded by acts of terror perpetrated by such Jewish activists as the Stern gang against British personnel,
airfields, railway yards and other strategic targets in Palestine and further
afield, including the assassination in Cairo in 1944 of the British Minister
of State for the Middle East, Lord Moyes. After the creation of the state
of Israel in 1948, the group, which had always been condemned by
moderate Jewish leaders, was suppressed.

The sense of Palestinian injustice has intensified through subsequent
wars where a series of Israeli victories have added to the Palestinian
sense of helplessness. The first Intifada, the Palestinian popular uprising
against the Israeli occupation of Palestinian territory, was in full flow

in October 1990 when we had a Christian Palestinian staying with us, and a script which I presented that month refers to efforts then being made, in spite of the violence, to cross the religious and political divides – 'Working for Reconciliation in Israel/Palestine'. In it I argued for grace and stamina. It proved to be mostly a vain hope, for ten years later very little progress had been made as I pointed out in the 'Thought' of 22 May 2001 'Ospreys and the Middle East'. And 9/11 was to occur three and a half months later.

WORKING FOR RECONCILIATION IN ISRAEL/PALESTINE, 10 OCTOBER 1990

A couple of weeks ago we had a Palestinian Christian from Israel staying with us. He said that he was pleased to be visiting Britain, even for only ten days, because it gave him a small break from the constant pressure upon him back home where he's been trying to build communities of peace and reconciliation in a deeply troubled land.

He said to us,. 'It's no good you British people going to the Middle East and saying that you've been walking where Jesus walked. I've been walking where Jesus walked for more than 50 years and there's nothing very special about that. What is special is meeting God in the people who still live in the land where Jesus lived – the Christian Palestinians, the Muslim Palestinians, and the Jews.' He went on, 'You people visit my country and come back knowing about every crack in every holy building, but you don't meet the people and hear their stories about the reality of their lives. Well he's probably back now and I don't know what he's making of the present reality of Muslims stoning Jews, Jews shooting Muslim, both groups claiming provocation by the other, and to cap it all the President of Iraq threatening to unleash missiles on Israel.'

At least through the visit of our friend I've learned that there are other realities in Israel and the occupied territories; that there are schools where children from all sections are being educated together, where arab children are learning Hebrew and Jewish children are learning Arabic;

that there are communities where blind people from across the divides find a common cause in their blindness; that there are groups dedicated to organizing programmes for teenagers – Jews, Muslims and Christians alike, so that they can make dramatic presentations pleading for understanding around the towns and villages, and so work to develop the land together.

From our visitor we learned then, that there are many people in all sections of the community who are working for peace and reconciliation and of course these are the ones who will have been most severely let down by the present outbreak of hostilities, and if we wouldn't care to be judged by some of the wilder statements and actions of extremist groups in our own land, perhaps we should beware of falling into the trap of judging the people of the Middle East by their extremists. But having said all that, the situation is both serious and confusing. There are times and situations where the only response of thoughtful outsiders is one of confusion and compassion, and it's no weakness to confess such. This would appear to be one such time and one such situation. I often use a prayer which asks that, where courage is needed to take hard decisions our souls might be steeled for the task, but where we need the patience to wait we might be given the grace and stamina to do so. I think that prayer is needed now.

And ten years later:

OSPREY AND THE MIDDLE EAST, 22 MAY 2001

Ospreys are nesting again in England probably for the first time in two centuries. I'm told that the osprey has a curious feature. It's talons are so designed that once it has grasped a fish it can't let it go until it's back on dry land. Of course there are obvious advantages in this. The bird can swoop down, snatch its prey from the water and be gone again in a flash without the danger of losing its catch. But there's a downside. What happens when the osprey grasps a fish that's too heavy? It can neither let it go, nor fly. You don't need me to dwell on the details of the possible scenarios: a wounded fish inseparably connected to a drowning bird. Neither is the winner.

Well, if ever there was a fish that was too big to fly with, the present conflict in the Middle East may very well be it with America being cast in the role of the osprey. Under President Clinton, America tried and tried to bring peace between Palestinian and Israeli. It couldn't let it go – but neither could it pull the conflict for any length of time out of the murky waters of violence, dispute and hatred and soar into the clear sky. President Bush's America, sensing danger, has hung back, until now.

Yesterday, the long-awaited Mitchell report was unveiled in New York. It's proposals are totally sensible – disengagement on both sides, a total freeze on Jewish settlements in Palestinian areas, clear statements by the Palestinian authorities for an end to all violence. Fine – but these proposals have long since been anticipated and rejected. So the call goes out once more for the American eagle or osprey to fly to the rescue and attempt a miracle of healing and the American Secretary of State, Colin Powell, agrees to appoint a mediator.

Jesus of Nazareth knew all about the frenzy of Middle Eastern politics; after all, he was Jesus of Nazareth then as now in the heart of turmoil and conflict. At one time he told his followers to love their enemies, at another he told them to be as wise as serpents and innocent as doves.

I suspect that both are relevant if the present situation is to be resolved. To love your enemy is no sentimental advice: it's the hard-headed way forward in conflict situations, particularly when the wells of hatred and suspicion run deep. But there's a long way to go before the Israelis and the Palestinians can even nudge in the direction of forgiveness and the new life that this brings with any conviction.

To do that they need help from their friends. They need mediators: not the osprey but the innocent dove and the wise serpent; both are needed if they're going to be released from their present hook where there's neither flight nor freedom.

Of course domestic developments were also colouring the cultural and religious mix in Britain and adding to a sense of dislocation of many in the British Islamic community. The most dramatic was the publication of the novel *The Satanic Verses* by Salmon Rushdie and the widespread reaction of outrage and even book burning with a fatwa issued in 1989 calling for the author's death. The fault line between outraged Muslims horrified at what they saw as a slur on the honour of the prophet Mohammed, and the liberal Western respect for free speech, became very clear. The Muslim call for the book to be banned was rejected and the outrage was intensified in October 1990 when the British Board of Film Classification refused to pass a Pakistani-made film showing Mr Rushdie as a debauched plotter against Islam. I presented a 'Thought' stressing the need for the wider community to support moderate Islamic leaders in Britain.

THE RUSHDI AFFAIR AND CENSORSHIP, 23 OCTOBER 1990

The Rushdi affair has been given another turn of the screw this week by the decision of the British Board of Film Classification to refuse to pass the Pakistani-made film which shows Mr Rushdie as a debauched plotter against Islam. And this time, I for one am firmly on the side of the Muslim community. The film board may be acting quite correctly within their technical guidelines, indeed they may be acting quite correctly within the law, but if so, then the law seems unfair.

Let's look as the affair as it might seem to the man on the top of the Bradford omnibus. Salmon Rushdie writes a book which Muslims believe treats the founder of their religion in an untrue and insulting way. Muslim leaders try to have the book banned and are told that this is not possible within British law. They are further told that it is their duty to keep any protests peacefully within the law. Fair enough. Then this film is made which, we're told, treats Salmon Rushdie in an untrue and insulting way, and immediately the film is banned, before the courts have even had a chance to decide whether or not it falls within the law. It really doesn't seem to add up to fair and even-handed treatment. It's not as if every docudrama at the cinema or on television about recent history pretends to true accuracy. We are well used to faction – the portrayal of real events concerning real people in such a way that fact overlaps with fiction – and from the snippets shown on the TV news this is clearly the style of the Pakistani film.

Of course there is the danger that such a film will inflame tensions further, but I believe that there is an even greater danger of giving ammunition to those wilder members of the Muslim community who would have us believe that British society is totally hostile to their religion. Now Christians wouldn't want their faith to be judged totally on statements emerging from some of the noisier leaders in Northern Ireland, and equally I believe that it's unfair to judge a great and civilized religion like Islam on the basis of statements from its more bigoted leaders. It's obvious that, as with Christianity, there are division within the Muslim community, and for every hard-line leader using rash and angry words, there are moderate leaders urging that Muslims should play a full and constructive part in the life of our country in an open and democratic way.

Such leaders are not helped if it seems that British laws and institutions are weighted against minority groups like their own. St Thomas Aquinas in his great study on law spoke of the Law of God, the law of justice and love, overarching all human laws. All societies have a duty to try to see that their human laws and institutions approximate to those of the Law of God, and benchmarks of good laws include balance, even-handedness and fairness. Traditionally, in this country, we pride ourselves on such values; we had better show that we still believe in them.

I returned to a similar theme in the more worrying days of 2004, some 14 years later. In my national role as a co-chair of the Inter Faith Network of Britain and Ireland, following the encouraging coming together of the faiths in the marking of the Millennium and the cooperation around the creation of the Spirit Zone in the Millennium Dome, I was becoming very anxious at the way that the shock of the 9/11 atrocities in New

York was leading to faith communities throughout Europe, including Britain, turning inward, with dangerous effects on community cohesion. The August 2004 script was in response to a French ban upon the wearing of Islamic headscarves. I didn't know it at the time of course, but it was delivered some 12 months before the bombs on the London Underground, the very thing which I had been fearing.

ISLAMIC HEADSCARVES, 31 AUGUST 2004

It's not yet clear whether the French foreign minister and other voices, including those of French Muslims, will be successful in saving the lives of the two French journalists threatened with death in Iraq unless the French government revokes the law banning all conspicuous displays of religious faith in state schools, which comes into force this week.

Every modern state has been faced with the question, 'How much freedom can a state give to the various faith and ethnic communities to express, symbolize and propagate their faith or culture whilst still keeping a unified and coherent state?' It's not only Muslims in France who are unhappy with the new law – Christians, Sikh and Jewish people have also protested – but the main energy of the protest has focused upon the freedom of some Muslim girls to wear an Islamic headscarf in school.

Different democracies have had different histories which have formed their present practices. For example, out of their particular historical struggle, France, Turkey and America exclude religion from formal expression in public life, whilst faith groups have protection to teach, express and propagate their faith privately. This causes some difficulty for Christians and Muslims in particular, who believe that there is no area of life which isn't affected by their faith, but it has to be said that Christian and Jewish people in America seem to have no difficulty in wielding significant influence on their political leaders.

British history has led us to a different pattern of public life. Through bloody struggles has evolved the pattern of a constitutional monarchy and constitutional religion with faith having a formal place in state institutions including schools. From bitter experience of earlier struggles between Christian denominations, however, we've learned that our pattern works best when all feel that their faith has an honourable place in national life, and I believe that in modern Britain it's possible for us all to be both proud and committed to our faith and culture, and to be citizens working together for the common good.

Our 30 medal winners at the Olympics came from many different faith and ethic groups. They were proud to be British and Britain was proud of them. But national cohesion depends also upon faith communities being reasonable in the demands that they make upon their fellow citizens. A woman Muslim head of a state comprehensive school whom I know will allow her girls, if they wish, to wear a headscarf as part of the school uniform, but she insists that there are perfectly good health and safety reasons why this must not obscure the face in any way.In an emergency, members of staff must be able to recognize instantly every pupil. She has no problems. Sometimes in faith as in other matters, an ounce of common sense is worth a ton of ideology.

But of course, as I have indicated, the attack on the Twin Towers in New York in the name of Islamic fundamentalism on 9/11 2001 had changed everything. A formerly seemingly impregnable USA now was shown to be vulnerable. The self-image of an America chosen to be a beacon of democracy and a centre of Christian civilization, to some 'The New Israel,' was threatened by an alternative view shared by the terrorist hijackers and those who supported them – that the USA was itself the source of evil. Through its worldwide exports of materialistic goods and cultural ideology, many in the Middle East and elsewhere saw their own culture, religion, economy, values and way of life under threat. Those embracing Islamism were determined to resist this and within those were people prepared to use violence and terrorism. From that mindset and perspective the Twin Towers of the World Trade Center was a symbol of that evil and so a legitimate target for attack.

The shock of the 9/11 terrorist atrocity was intensified by the fact that the most highly developed intelligence agencies on earth provided no warning of such an attack. The heroism of fire-fighters, police and ordinary citizens in response to the attack was inspiring but nothing could erase the images of people jumping to their deaths from the skyscrapers rather than burn to death.

The reaction to 9/11 was dramatic, immediate and long-lasting. The 'War on Terror' had begun. It intensified the American and British determination to suppress Al Qaeda terror training camps in Afghanistan; it motivated President Bush – with support from British Prime Minister Tony Blair – to invade Iraq; and it was to lead to copycat Islamist terrorist attacks in European cities including London.

The fear of this kind of scenario was in my mind when I presented, ten days after 9/11, the 'Thought' 'Action and Reaction', with its final plea, 'Refusing to over-react needn't smell of appeasement; it might be the first step down the road to a more costly justice.' Perhaps, with nerves and emotions at the time being so raw, it was inevitably a plea which was not to be heeded.

ACTION AND REACTION, 17 SEPTEMBER 2001

You'll remember from your school science the Newtonian law of physics that for every action there is an equal and opposite reaction. We've had recent experience of it in the remarkable foot bridge across the River Thames, which closed soon after it opened. It was underdamped and the law of action and reaction led to ever extending lurches from side to side until everyone was sick. Extensive damping to reduce the oscillations has had to be provided so that people can walk across the bridge in stability and peace.

What's true of the material world it seems to me is also true in the world of emotions, in the world of debate, and it can even be true in the world of international affairs. Then the danger is very real indeed for violent provocation leads to a violent response which in turn leads to an even more violent act of retribution which is met with yet more sickening and amplified atrocity. So any high moral ground is soon lost in the morass of accusation and counter-accusation whilst the number of innocent victims multiply. We can't yet know what America will do in the face of last Tuesday's atrocity; much will depend on whether the Taliban hand over Osama Bin Laden but I for one have a sense of foreboding.

And terror makes victims of us all. The repercussions of Tuesday's events are already being felt in our own land. We're not in a position to influence what decisions might be made on this in a damaged Pentagon but we all have some responsibility for how the ripples of repercussion affect our own communities. We have a part to play in damping down the rhetoric and fear here in Britain so that community, race and faith relationships aren't further damaged.

We mustn't be silent when our fellow Islamic citizens live in fear when the ignorant associate them with Muslim fanatics. Christians like myself wouldn't be pleased if we were judged on the basis of the wilder atrocities committed by Catholic or Protestant paramilitaries over the years and equally we mustn't judge adherents of other noble world faiths by their more fanatical believers.

Wisely, President Bush visited an Islamic centre yesterday and spoke of religions sharing the same values of respect. The truth is that religion can encourage its more fanatical adherents into increasingly inflammatory words and actions. Yet it can also bring peace and balance by damping out the oscillations of action and reaction. Jesus Christ taught his followers: don't react; do good to those who hate you; be generous, not mean; be merciful. Change the pattern of behaviour even if it means refusing to react when your own people hate you, even if you end up on a cross.

Refusing to over-react needn't smell of appeasement: it might be the first step down the road to a more costly justice.

The previous chapter covered some of the international action and reaction to the 'War on Terror' and of course these continue with unfinished business in the war against the Taliban in Afghanistan. It is beginning to become clear to all sides that, as with the engagement with the IRA and Protestant terrorists in Northern Ireland no purely military victory is likely or indeed possible and that any solution is going to include political negotiations. The road ahead might well still be long and arduous before a legitimate national government, able to take forward the hoped for developments in education and social justice, is in place and the allied forces are able to withdraw with confidence. What is a abundantly clear is that such a national government will need to involve members of the Taliban, which at this stage show all the signs of being 'a government in waiting'.

But this chapter focuses more on the reaction to the War on Terror here in Britain. Earlier in the chapter I suggested that there seems to be three ingredients feeding modern movements of terror. First, there is this progression from a traditional faith to a more fundamentalist form and then to its violent expression. Secondly, there is a political ingredient where terror is seen as the sole weapon for a people's perceived oppression. Thirdly, there is often something going on in the personal lives of the recruits to terrorism.

In the case of Islam we have seen networks of believers moving from being devout orthodox Muslims to Islamists with an active religious and political motivation, and then for some an activism dedicated to violence and terror. The political ingredient in the mix of terror was fed by the perceived long-standing favouritism of the West for Israel in the Israeli–Palestinian disputes, followed by the invasion of Iraq and Afghanistan, with President Bush, foolishly using the word 'crusade'. All this fed the message of Islamism that Islam was under attack around the globe and that the attack must be resisted – a jihad or holy war must be undertaken. Then it was claimed that with the Western powers and their puppet Islamic regimes having a virtual monopoly in modern weaponry, the use of terror, including suicide bombing, was legitimate and even noble. Suicide is a sin in Islam, but in the context of jihad can be justified and even commended, for to lay down one's life fighting the enemies of Islam is not suicide but martyrdom. The London bombings of 7/7 2005 were a typical action of those believing this teaching.

Three young men drove from Leeds and met up with a fourth at Luton. From there they took the train to Kings Cross station where closed circuit TV cameras recorded them embracing one another and then going off in separate directions carrying rucksacks which we now know contained explosives. At 8.50 a.m. at the height of the rush hour three of the terrorists detonated their bombs on Underground trains: at Aldgate where seven people were killed; at Edgware killing six; and at Russell Square killing 26. The fourth bomber seems to have had problems with his arrangements and so took a double-decker bus where he detonated his bomb in Tavistock Square, killing 13 people. In all, 52 people were killed and 770 were injured.

It took five years before the inquests on the fatalities opened but some facts soon became obvious. What was first regarded as an electricity supply failure was quite quickly seen as a series of serious incidents. The scale and number of the attacks seemed to cause great confusion for the rescue services and their equipment. As the wounded began to emerge telling their stories it was obvious, however, that individual members of London Underground staff, together with individual police officers, fire-fighters and fellow passengers, had been heroic in trying to save the lives of grievously wounded people. The response of the community was predictable. London faith and civic leaders gathered in a ceremony to honour the dead and bereaved and to express their determination to stand together against such horror. Lessons are still being learned, however, and the later inquest revealed that there were serious systemic weaknesses in coordinating the responses and the equipment of all the rescue services.

The British government had been working to build community cohesion and to protect British citizens from terrorist attacks. In response to 7/7 it now drafted a new Terrorism Bill and presented it to Parliament in November 2005. I happened to be presenting a 'Thought for the Day', on 22 November, the day the bill reached the House of Lords. In it I focused on the developed just war criteria of necessity and proportionality. Restricting the rights of its citizens, particularly in an emergency, might well be the duty of any government, but the restriction must be proportionate to the perceived threat. Furthermore, because draconian actions might weigh disproportionately heavily on minority groups within the community, these might even increase the threat of further terrorism.

TERRORISM DEBATE, 22 NOVEMBER 2005

The House of Lords yesterday began examining the governments Terrorism Bill and not surprisingly the atmosphere was grave. The London bombings of 7 July have confirmed that our nation faces a serious challenge which – despite our prolonged experience of IRA terrorism – has significantly new features. The international origins of the threat, the loosely organized groups who lie low with destructive intent, and the use of suicide bombers, present new problems to our police and security services. But the challenge isn't only one of detection or prevention. The strategies and policies we adopt in response will affect the character of our society.

One of the most disturbing meetings which I have recently attended was with a senior London police officer. It was obvious that in his mind, it wasn't a question as to whether there would be another terrorist attack in London, the question was simply, 'When would it happen?' If that is so, and if such attacks are very difficult to prevent without much more intensive intelligence, then it's understandable that any government would want to send clear signals to the public that it was doing every-thing possible to prevent an attack. The danger of this is that draconian measures might be proposed which in themselves undermine the way of life of a civilized democracy. None of us wants to be accused the day after an attack of failing in our civic duty, but part of our duty is to keep a sense of proportion in considering fresh legislation.

Traditional ethical criteria would suggest that any proposal to restrict rights and liberties should be assessed by the criteria of necessity – is it likely to work, and is there any other way of doing it? – and proportion-ality – is the restriction comparable in scale with the threat it seeks to forestall? The problem then is how to weigh various risks against one another.

Part of the response must be a political strategy that engages with Muslim perceptions of injustice in the United Kingdom and across the world. We must get beyond portraying ourselves, or anyone else, as purely innocent victims of other people's wrongdoings and therefore beyond criticism. Christians are aware that all human beings are trapped in historical and socially-transmitted patterns of harm, fear, suspicion and sin.

The experience of the Christian Church is that in a fallen world, understanding and reconciliation are attainable only by engagement – that is, through perceptiveness, hard thinking, repentance, courage and costly effort in openness to others. The challenge of terrorism isn't just to government but to every citizen in seeking a way of life which reflects the justice, compassion and perseverance of God.

Five years on, we are in a better position to gain some understanding of what might have led British-born young men – one of them, the leader, a devoted husband with a new baby – to leave home one morning and kill themselves and others in a carefully planned terrorist attack.

The three ingredients feeding modern movements of terror all seem to have been there in their cases. First, there was the progression from a traditional faith to a more fundamentalist form. Three of the four bombers came from Beeston in inner city Leeds, from a tight-knit traditional Islamic Pakistani community. They worshipped with their families in the local mosque and went to local schools and colleges. A factor providing the seedbed for change was the advent of drugs and drug pushers into the community. The traditional community leaders seemed helpless in the face of such an invasion. The later bombers sought a more activist expression of the Islamic faith and found it in an Islamist Wahhabi-inclined mosque. They joined a group of second-generation Pakistanis called the 'Mullah boys', formed in the mid-1990s initially as a response to the drug issue. According to those who knew them well, the group would even kidnap young addicts and forcibly clean them of their drug habits. Initially the radicalized faith of the young men was welcomed by the older generation in Beeston, but fractures between the generations soon began to appear: they were religious, political, and personal.

The older generation formed a cohesive and partially ghettoized community, having their origin in rural Pakistan where the rules of tradition are strict and unforgiving, and where the structures of justice, security and social support are organized by the local tribe and not the central state. In Britain these traditional leaders were more comfortable working hard, bringing up their children and encouraging them to marry tribal friends or relations and 'keeping themselves to themselves' and separate from wider British society. This was not an option for the second-generation young men being educated in British schools and colleges, and many, like the later bombers, found themselves no longer fitting into their traditional families and community, but neither did they feel that they were totally accepted in British society.

They found a new family, community and faith in the Islamist mosque with its global connections, stressing solidarity with the 'Umma', the notion of an Islamic nation or people who accept the core beliefs of Islam, true Muslims everywhere. With this perception the plight of Muslims elsewhere in the world, particularly those in the Middle East, became the concern and responsibility of the true believer and so the second, political, ingredient began to come strongly to the fore and with it the use of terror, seen as the weapon to fight for the rights of oppressed Muslims.

A third and more personal element also appeared with the Islamism. Unlike the traditional, tribal faith of their parents stressing the duty of marriage within the extended family, an Islamist was free to marry any Muslim from any part of the world. When the future bombers began to marry their own choice of partner this was a further serious personal rift with their families putting them even more firmly into the Islamist sect. The ingredients of the terrorist were now all in place: the move from a traditionalist Islam to a radicalized Islamist faith; a sense of isolation from society together with a sense of solidarity with oppressed Muslims; a belief that the weapon of terror was legitimate and even noble to combat the oppression; and a personal call to give one's own life in the battle. Of course there was the additional belief that such an action for the faith would result in a future life in paradise and so they would soon be eternally reunited with families and friends. And so, according to the official account of 7/7, at around 8.30 a.m. at Kings Cross station 'four men fitting their descriptions are seen hugging one another … They appear happy, even euphoric.'

Five years later, to the day, I presented a 'Thought' touching on some of this.

7/7 FIFTH ANNIVERSARY, 7 JULY 2010

This is a day for commemoration and reflection. We commemorate the victims of the 7/7 outrage five years ago and show deep sympathy for those whose lives have been wounded by bereavement or injury. But this is also a time of reflection. How could four young men, bred and educated in Britain, give each other a warm hug outside Kings Cross station and then go and destroy themselves and their fellow Underground passengers? Three of the four came from Beeston, not far away from this Leeds studio, and so, naturally, nowhere has the soul searching and the bewilderment been greater than in the traditional Pakistani community trying to live decent lives in this city. Indeed the Leeds Makkah Mosque this afternoon is seeking to commemorate 7/7 by sponsoring an inter-faith conference, 'Communities United'. I hope to be there.

For we're all involved in this because if four such unlikely revolutionaries could be recruited and trained for terror without family and community being aware or overconcerned then who else might be going through the process at the moment? It might be fruitful to unscramble some of the ingredients that fed into 7/7. One might have been the tensions present in their community when the young men were growing up, particularly the serious racial unrest in Oldham, Bradford and Leeds in 2001.

Then it's not surprising if there's confusion over identity. I know from the many discussions I've had when I was national co-chair of the Inter Faith Network seeking to find common ground between the faiths that so many of the core tenets we believe are rooted in peace, care for neighbour, and personal identity. But who is such a young man to be? A loyal and obedient son of hard working parents living lives shaped in the traditional culture of rural Pakistan, or does he truly belong in the Britain that has educated him, but where he's not finding it easy to fit in?

Young men and women living out their lives on such an overlap are ripe for exploitation by any group which gives clear leadership, which offers a message claiming to give meaning to confused lives, and which offers a cause which gives the recruit status and a place in a cadre of colleagues. And if this is accompanied by extremist religious teaching – dramatically different from mainstream Islam – and a sense of outrage that, globally, fellow believers are being persecuted, then, sadly this is potentially a dangerous package.

And the answer? Patience and persistence. Invest in intelligence gathering and work together to build a just compassionate society where none are excluded. And there are good stories to tell, none better than the meeting last night of a hundred orthodox Jewish and devout Muslim women coming together to foster closer ties between their communities. It is such a gathering that can mark the start towards a more constructive future.

What should be the reaction of political and faith communities to this? The New Labour British government was not inactive. Within a policy of CONTEST, a UK counter-terrorism strategy was developed with the elements of 'Pursue', stopping terrorist attacks; 'Prevent', stopping people becoming terrorists; 'Protect', strengthening protection against attacks; and 'Prepare', where an attack cannot stopped, to mitigate its effects. In Britain, at least, the first two elements of the strategy tended to work against each other. The British government might have seen the wars in Afghanistan and Iraq as being part of the 'Pursue' element, destroying potential domestic terrorist training and support, but for many moderate Muslims in the UK there was anger at what appeared to be a US/UK attack on Muslim countries. The second element, the 'Prevent' strategy, aimed at combating the radicalization of young Muslims received a mixed reception.

The five objectives of 'Prevent' were stated as being to: challenge the ideology behind violent extremism and support mainstream voices; disrupt those who promote violent extremism and support the places where they operate; support individuals who are vulnerable to recruitment or who have already been recruited by violent extremists; increase the resilience of communities to violent extremism; and to address the grievances which ideologues are exploiting.

Money followed policy. The Preventing Violent Extremism Pathfinder Fund was launched in October 2006 to support priority local authority areas in developing programmes of activity to tackle violent extremism through the work of the local Prevent partnerships. The fund made £6 million available to 70 priority local authorities 'to build on their existing work to engage with their local communities, forge partnerships with police, community and faith groups, and to work with mosques and institutions of education'. In October 2007 it was announced that a further £45 million funding was to be given to 82 local authorities to allow the broadening of work on Prevent and the funding of projects in their areas.

A further development explained that while the focus of the Prevent strategy was to be at the local level, the government has also funded a number of national programmes which are aimed specifically at combating extremism within Muslim communities. These include the 'Contextualising Islam in Britain' project in which the University of Cambridge leads a group of academics and scholars. The guidance says that 'it is not the role of the Government to intervene directly in matters of faith. But where theology purports to justify and legitimize violent extremism, the Government will work with communities and institutions who are best placed to refute it and to provide a coherent response to the questions it may pose.'

It was this targeting of the Muslim community and agencies which had a mixed reception both within the Islamic communities and other faith and secular groups. As always when people and agencies are competing for public funding, there was talk about bias and other religious faith leaders in Britain, such as Hindu and Sikh leaders, found it difficult to explain to some of their followers why Muslim groups in inner city areas such as theirs were seemingly being favoured in grant aid. Then within the Muslim community not every moderate group or mosque was happy to accept government money which they felt might affect their independence or compromise their stance on public and religious matters.

Five years later, and with a new government in office, the Prevent programme is being reassessed and it will be interesting to see what can be learned from this brave attempt at building community cohesion.

The 'Protect' element mostly consisted from 1998 of taking a series of Anti-Terrorism Acts through Parliament; six were put on the statute books before New Labour lost office. They successively proscribed terrorist organizations and confiscated their property; brought in control orders on those suspected of planning terrorism; brought in new offences for encouraging terrorism and disseminating terrorist publications including internet activity; and extended the period a suspect could be held in detention without charge to 28 days (the government had wanted this to be 90 days). Much of this legislation ran into trouble when tested in the courts but it signalled the seriousness of British political leaders in combating domestic terrorism.

This legislation was undergirded by a strengthening of the intelligence agencies, but the difficulties they were having in receiving accurate intelligence from a partially alienated community was well illustrated in a high-profile siege of a house in Forest Gate in June 2006. Here, armed police, acting on what they described at the time as specific intelligence indicating that the inhabitants might be in possession of chemical weapons, arrested two men. Nothing was found and the men were shortly released without charge. Such actions, of course, did not help the 'Prevent' element of the anti-terrorism strategy nor assist the task of community cohesion.

It is in this latter task that religious people in Britain might have a significant part to play. Whilst also recognizing the genuine political issues, Christian people in particular have a responsibility to seek to understand some of the faith complexities and pressures of modern Islam. We should recognize and help Muslims to communicate the fact that most Muslims would want to distinguish between 'Muslims', 'Islamists' and 'Islamist terrorists'. Indeed the latter group are more akin to earlier terrorist cells of the 1970s and 1980s having no religious affiliation – for example, the Baader-Meinhof gang, the Red Brigades, and extremist versions of Marxist-Leninism. Such terrorism in the name of Islam is a total perversion and betrayal of orthodox Islam. The fact that one might be able to understand the process of a young man or woman becoming a terrorist of the anarchist Red Brigades, or of the Islamist variety, however, does not mean that such terrorism must not be firmly resisted.

Theological dialogue has a part to play in this. The Qur'an is regarded by Muslims as the very words of God communicated to the Prophet Mohammed but needs to be interpreted by Muslims in the wide variety of different contexts today, a process which has hardly begun. For example, in the Qur'an there is a wide range of attitudes expressed towards Christians – some very positive, others hostile and critical – and Muslims need to work out principles of interpretation to show which of these verses are most relevant in their relationships with Christians today.

It also needs to be recognized that there is a fierce debate taking place within contemporary Islam over the nature of 'jihad' in a context where one in four Muslims around the world are living as minority communities in pluralistic societies. 'Jihad' means 'struggle', but is this to be interpreted as the religious obligation of all true Muslims – to join the jihad to promote a global Islamic revolution, as the Islamists claim – or should Muslims adopt a more spiritual meaning, of a struggle for right-eousness, as many moderate Muslim leaders in the West have done in recent years?

There is an equally important debate going on within Islam on the question of violence. Muslims generally have no hesitation in saying that war and violence are justified in self-defence and so Muslims and Islamic nations have the right to defend themselves. Islamic law lays down clear guidelines for the conduct of war with similarities to the Christian concept of the just war as discussed in the previous chapter. There are deep divisions regarding the legitimacy of the use of terror, however. Islamists engaged in terrorism regard the use of violence as a legitimate application of Islamic beliefs and values; other Muslims, however, argue that such violence is totally unacceptable because it goes against Islamic 'Shari'a' which forbids violence against civilians. The late Dr Zaki Badawi of the Muslim College in London wrote in response to 9/11: 'Those who plan and carry out such acts are condemned by Islam, and the massacre of thousands, whoever perpetrated it, is a crime against God as well as humanity.' Islamic leaders who take this approach then are saying that terror in the name of Islam is a total betrayal of real Islam.

The domestic struggle against terrorism in Britain then is by no means over. Christians in Britain can probably best help by recognizing the international and domestic actions which, if disproportionate, make the task of moderate Muslims of holding their community within mainstream British society more difficult. It is not helpful when wilder Christian voices claim that the Qur'an is essentially violent, or that Islam is basically a violent religion. Indeed, Christians should be willing to support those Muslims who challenge the harsher and more violent interpretations of the Qur'an. The important thing to recognize is that this challenge, if it is to be fruitful, must take place within Islam, and Muslims must have the space to do so.

Christians have an important role to play in relating faith to the demands of community life in a secular pluralistic society such as Britain. For over a hundred years Christians in the West have known the distress and confusion of its holy book, the Bible, coming under hostile forensic scrutiny, but if anything, the result has been a strengthening and deepening of Christian understanding. Muslims have nothing to fear in discussing and debating amongst themselves the interpretation of their scriptures in a society such as ours. Then in recent years it has become clear that many British political leaders and civil servants have little personal awareness of religious faith. They are not necessarily hostile to religion; they simply don't have a world view or language to understand where Christians or indeed Muslims are coming from. Such influential people are prepared to give religion an honoured place in private life but neither Christianity nor Islam is content with this for both see their faith as having an important part to play in public life. Since 9/11, in my role as co-chair of the Inter Faith Network and a bishop in the House of Lords, I have been constantly engaged in the process of education, not so much between the religious faiths but between those with a firm public faith rooted in belief in God, and those, the majority of our legislators, whose understanding is secular-rooted in the culture of human rights. This dialogue goes to the heart of our common life and is essential if terrorism is to be eliminated from our nation.

3

Religion and Politics

Both religion and politics seek to serve the common good and so it is not surprising if, from time to time, there is an overlap. We have seen at different times in history, particularly at the Reformation, political life in Europe driven by religious disputes. England saw a civil war where religious attitudes again shaped the various participants. Again in our own time, the collapse of communism has created a vacuum which Islam is filling as an alternative ideology to Western globalization. It is no wonder that many politicians regard religion with suspicion, knowing that its influence can have unpredictable results. Equally, religious people can be disturbed by the power wielded by political leaders, not always for the common good, and the ease with which politicians can be deluded or delude themselves when the real motive is the desire for political advancement. A 'Thought' in May 1991 was triggered by a contrary decision, the refusal of Sonia Gandhi to become president of the Congress party after her husband had been assassinated.

POMP AND POWER, 27 MAY 1991

Latest reports from India suggest that the Congress party has stopped trying to persuade Sonia Gandhi to become its president in her husband's place following his assassination. The attempt to appoint her president has reminded me of the story of the group of ambassadors who were once sent by the Emperor of China to a certain hermit living in the northern mountains. They were to invite him to become prime minister of the kingdom.

After many days of travel they arrived to find the hermitage empty, but nearby in the middle of the river was a half-naked man fishing.

Inquiries at the village proved that this was the man of whom the Emperor thought so highly. When the hermit waded ashore the chief ambassador spoke, 'Honoured sir, his majesty the Emperor, having heard of your wisdom and your holiness, has sent us with these gifts. He invites you to accept the post of prime minister of the realm. 'Is his majesty out of his mind?' roared the hermit with uncontrollable laughter. Then he said, 'Tell me, is it true that mounted over the main altar of the Emperor's chapel is a stuffed turtle whose shell is encrusted with sparkling diamonds and to whom the Emperor and his household gather to do homage?' 'It is, venerable sir' they replied. 'Now' he said, 'take this turtle here wagging his tail in the mud, do you think that this poor little fellow would change places with that turtle in the palace?' 'No he would not,' they replied. 'Then go and tell the Emperor that neither will I. For no one can be truly alive on a pedestal.'

The great religions of the world are suspicious of both pomp and power. Pomp separated from power, like the jewel encrusted turtle, is empty and lifeless and those put on public pedestals pay a great human price for the worship and flattery they receive. Power, however, the religions teach, is not meant to be the preserve of a few, but it is a gift from God to the whole of humanity to better order the life of the world. Those who carry power and position should be conscious that they carry it on behalf of others and must be ready both to exercise it, or lay it down, for the common good.

In the Christian religion the sign of authority and power looks nothing like a jewel encrusted turtle. It's a cross on a hillside upon which the man who refused to be king lay down his life so that others might live. Somewhere in the grief and powerlessness of that event lies the strength which destroys the powers which would dehumanize us. Just as in the quiet dignity and pain of Sonia Gandhi and her family in the face of their appalling personal tragedy, we see more hope for humanity than in all the frantic activity of the politicians desperately seeking to appoint a replacement for a lost leader. True strength and authority surely lies with *the grieving woman who knows that life on a pedestal is no life for her and has the courage to say 'No' to it.*

After a time out of politics Sonia Gandhi agreed to stand as president of the Congress party in 1998. She was elected and then was re-elected four times, becoming the longest serving president the party had ever had. This perhaps is a good example of the advice for the author of Ecclesiastes that there is a right time for everything, in this case a time to withdraw from political life and a time to engage in it, but if Church leaders engage then they can expect to receive criticism, particularly if their intervention has effect. The most common criticism is, 'Bishops shouldn't involve themselves in politics; they should get on with teaching the Bible in church.' I rather sympathize with Archbishop Desmond Tutu's response to that. He simply said, 'I don't know what Bible they are reading.'

The Bible, of course is full of politics although the Old Testament and the New Testament take different perspectives. In the Old Testament the people of Israel at different times were slaves, asylum seekers, in exile, running their own affairs and living in an occupied land. How to serve the common good in this varied and various set of situations was not always clear, but throughout the covenant between God and his people took central stage. When kings of Israel or Judah had their hands on the levers of power the prophets would remind them of the covenant and challenge them to serve with justice and walk with humility. When the people were in exile or enslaved in their own land the message was one of hope: the God who had been faithful to the covenant in the past would be faithful in the future.

The members of the early Church were nowhere near the levers of power. Roman power was at its zenith. By the time the bulk of the New Testament had been written the temple at Jerusalem had been destroyed and the Jewish people scattered throughout the empire and beyond. Christians were either scattered with them or had already been living in the towns and cities around the Mediterranean. They were always at the mercy of the civic authorities and it was not surprising if much of the time they sought to be good citizens and not draw attention to themselves. There were times, however, when it was impossible to do this without denying the faith, and martyrdom was endured. This proved to be the life-blood of the Church as many were impressed by the stead-fastness and courage of those who went to their deaths still praising their God. It would be several centuries before, under Constantine, the Church became the official religion of the empire, which would bring another set of challenges.

Given this varied and various history I find it helpful, developing the teaching of Richard Niebuhr on Christ and culture, to categorize the various attitudes which the Church may take to the state and its political life. A case for each can be argued from biblical teaching and subsequent Church history. These are 'The Church of the State', 'The Church Against the State', 'The Church and State Separated', 'The Church Above the State', 'The Church the Transformer of the State'. Each model has its strengths and weaknesses.

The strength of 'The Church of the State' is that religion is thoroughly incarnated in public life with opportunities for mission, service and influence for the common good. The Church of England as the estab-lished Church of the land, with bishops in the House of Lords, and with its parishes covering every square inch of land, each with a parish church and a resident vicar, is an example of this model. For over a decade, reform of the House of Lords has been on the political agenda including the place, if any, of bishops in a reformed chamber. Bishops make a particular contribution to debates, not only trying to contribute theological or spiritual input, but also their day-by-day experience of visiting schools, hospitals, prisons and other institutions in their dioceses. Their contribution is generally well received and there will be loss if the bishops were removed or their numbers dramatically reduced in a reformed house. To seriously follow a bill through all its stages in the House of Lords can take up to five days, perhaps scattered over a month. No bishop can set aside this amount of time in an already crowded diary and so bishops in the Lords usually work in teams specializing in education, prisons, foreign affairs and so on, so that if there is a major bill at least one bishop, knowledgeable on the subject, can be present for all of its stages. Only in this way can bishops seriously engage in helping to frame legislation. This 'Thought' of January 2003 was presented before one of the debates on Lords reform.

FUTURE OF THE HOUSE OF LORDS, 21 JANUARY 2003

A news item caught my eye yesterday concerning origami, the thousand-year-old Japanese art of paper folding. I'd always thought of it as a cute way of folding birds and paper aeroplanes, but apparently there's more to it than that. It now lies behind the optimum design for folding airbags inside a car's steering column or unfolding the photo-electric sails which power the instruments on satellites orbiting the earth. The secret is in the folding, and the folding, long since regarded as an art, is now also a science. An Italian mathematician has produced six axioms, which, with the help of a computer, can design and create the most wonderful of shapes with elegance and economy.

I was brooding on this as I sat listening to the two-day debate in the House of Lords concerning its own future. Ninety-three peers have put their names down to speak so nobody will be going home early tonight . I remember towards the end of an earlier debate marathon a peer getting to his feet and saying, 'Everything that could conceivably be said on this subject has been said. But it has not been said by me!' He then proceeded to say it all over again.

Hopefully today's debate will not be so gruelling if the House can take the example of origami and ask itself, 'What are the basic axioms from which an upper chamber for Parliament can be designed for today and tomorrow?' One axiom must surely be whether or not members would be elected or appointed, or whether the chamber would be composed of some hybrid. That's not an easy axiom. A totally elected chamber could lead to a elected dictatorship if both the Commons and the new upper house had the same large majority for the ruling party. Or if the upper house had a majority of the party in opposition in the Commons then the upper house might feel it legitimate to block any piece of legislation on the basis that it too had the legitimacy of the electorate. Of course an appointed house in total or part has different if equivalent dangers. Who does the appointing? On what basis? For how long?

But the composition of the upper chamber is only one axiom. Others involve the way it goes about its business, the hidden folds of committee and questioning through which legislation is scrutinized and revised and ministers are held accountable for their decisions. In a modern Parliament, what goes on in the debating chamber is only a small part of the work of its members.

It's probably no exaggeration to say that between them, St Augustine in the fourth century and St Thomas Aquinas in the thirteenth, shaped Western political thought. If Augustine's notion of The City of God caught the mindset of his era then Aquinas's Christian idea of governance as being for the common good I believe still has energy today. Whatever the other axioms might turn out to be, 'governance for the common good' is basic. Without it we might think we're designing a humming bird, but it will turn out to be an albatross.

The days have long gone when the Church of England, as the established Church of the nation, was characterized as 'the Tory party at prayer', or at least, 'the ruling party at prayer'. If there was any doubt that things had changed the publication of *Faith in the City* in 1985 removed them. Indeed, one government minister of the day called it a 'Marxist document' which of course helped to swell its sales and influence such as the establishment of the Church Urban Fund. No political party was focusing on the plight of the inner cities in 1985, but by the time of the next general election the issue was in every manifesto. Overall, the weakness of 'The Church of the State' model is that the distinctive challenge of the Christian message can be lost within the prevailing attitudes and mores of the society of the day. *Faith in the City*, sponsored by the then Archbishop of Canterbury Robert Runcie, however, demonstrated that

'The Church of the State' can sometimes adopt a more prophetic mode. The archbishop, himself decorated for bravery in the Second World War, had demonstrated moral bravery when he led the service in St Paul's Cathedral in June 1982 marking the end of the Falklands War, during which he insisted, much to the reported annoyance of Margaret Thatcher, the prime minister, that those bereaved and injured on all sides, including those of the Argentinian armed forces, should be included in the prayers. In fact these incidents during the leadership of Robert Runcie indicated that the Church of England was moving away from the traditional uncritical 'Church of the State' model and was beginning to demonstrate that an established Church can exist in critical solidarity with the state, whilst maintaining its own distinctive faith stance.

'The Church Against the State' has its roots in the persecution of the early Church by civic leaders such as Nero. The Church builds wall around itself and has very clear doctrines and beliefs often very different from those of the world around. The strength of this position is that there is little danger of the faith been watered down; the weakness is the likelihood of the Church becoming a sect with little influence on the world around and a tendency to internally divide and subdivide as the 'pure' gospel is sought and defended.

'The Church and State Separated', following some of the teaching of St Paul, sees both Church and state having God-given authority but in different spheres of life. Christians should be loyal and obedient to civic authorities, provided they in turn respect the internal life of the Church. Traditionally this has been the attitude of the Lutheran Church but its weakness was seen in Nazi Germany when the mainstream Church, until very late in the day, had not the theology or the tools to confront a state going badly wrong. Indeed, the separation of powers was such that the Church continued to accept the traditional Church tax even though it was Hitler's government which was collecting it and passing it on to the Church.

We see the best example of 'The Church Above the State' in the monasteries of medieval Europe where an alternative, and better, society was modelled. At its best the round of worship and work was uplifting and inspiring and the social work of the monks and nuns was impressive but the weakness of this model in England was the neglect of the spirituality and challenge of ordinary life, which left an overpowerful state when the monasteries were destroyed. There is still a natural yearning for this 'otherworldly' Church through such instruments as the Latin Mass, the Book of Common Prayer and the King James Bible (which even on publication, although in English, was devised to have a traditionalist feel).

This yearning is not confined to the British. I had an indication of the power of this pull when working as a missionary in Zambia. The first missionaries to Zambia were made welcome by the first tribe they met. They established a mission station and built a church, clinic and school. After some years they also translated the New Testament and the prayer book into Chinsenga, the local language. Later still they moved on further into the heart of the country and to their horror discovered that nobody else spoke Chinsenga. But the prayer book and the Bible had been translated into this language and these were the books that were used. A hundred years later, when we arrived, Chinsenga was still the worshipping language of the Anglican Church throughout Zambia. Some of the young Zambian priests were suggesting that the books should now be translated into the languages that people actually spoke, but there was furious resistance. Chinsenga was God's special language, it was claimed; they did not want to worship in the language of the market-place. An other-worldly Church still has great attraction to many people of all cultures.

The Church as the 'Transformer of the State' has its roots in the Old Testament prophets. To interact with the state, the Church has to be close enough to state power to have influence, but unlike the 'Church of the State' model it tries to keep its distinctive nature and message clear, not so much in an other-worldly or judgemental way, as with some of the other models, but in a genuine attempt to work with political life in the service of the common good. It is this model which has mostly formed my own thinking and lies behind much of the contributions of my 'Thoughts' to political life.

I am also cautious of the supposed certainties of party political life. I find it helpful, rather than taking a totally right or wrong approach to an issue, ideology or political programme, to first ask; what in this can be supported from Christian understanding; what in this must be opposed; what in this can be lived with, as seemingly being neutral to Christian values? Not everything must be fought tooth and nail, and not everything should be supported uncritically. If Christian leaders choose to enter into the hurly-burly of public debate they have a duty to be discriminating.

This approach is illustrated in a 'Thought' from November 1988 when Margaret Thatcher was still prime minister.

WHAT I WANT FROM POLITICIANS, 1 NOVEMBER 1988

It's the season of party conferences. When the Archbishop of Canterbury opened the Lambeth Conference at the beginning of the summer he told of a speaker whose speech was being interpreted. The speaker stopped every quarter on an hour for the interpreter to translate. After the first quarter the interpreter only seemed to say one sentence. The same thing happened after half and hour. After three-quarters of an hour there was a further single sentence. Then at the end of the speech the interpreter spoke a few more words and everyone applauded. The speaker was rather puzzled by all this and asked a friend how the interpreter had managed to condense the hour-long speech into four short sentences. 'Well,' said his friend, 'after you'd been speaking for a quarter of an hour the interpreter said, "He hasn't said anything yet." After half an hour he said, "He still hasn't said anything." After three-quarters of an hour he said, "I don't think he's going to say anything." And at the conclusion of your talk he said, "I told you so." Then they all started clapping.'

Perhaps it's as well that there aren't interpreters at party conferences for, as you know, when a bishop isn't talking he's not listening, and I suspect that that goes for politicians too. I sympathize with the chairman at one party conference who complained, 'Every time I try to get you all to take a decision, someone makes a speech.' I wouldn't mind that so much if the speeches weren't all so black and white. I often find myself wanting none of the social medicines on offer.

For example, the fact that I want decent housing for myself and my family doesn't mean that I want to see others sleeping rough under bridges. The fact that I want to be supportive to single teenage mothers in my city doesn't mean that I think that a stable marriage is not a great blessing. The fact that I'm prepared to pay my taxes to provide a decent health service doesn't mean that I want to live in some sort of Marxist cooperative. The fact that I enjoy the convenience of using a credit card doesn't mean that I want to be blown backwards and forwards by the financial winds of the City of London, nor that I want the freedom to run up debts far beyond my capacity to repay.

I want to live in a compassionate society, where my freedom of choice doesn't mean that someone else has an absence of choice; a society where people can develop their natural gifts and enjoy the fruits of their labours without inequalities growing to such an extent that my sense of decency and morality is offended; a society which looks after its own without forgetting that it's part of a world community.

I'm glad that I'm not a politician. The only comfort which I can bring to them in their conference season is that God knows that he's taken a risk in creating the world, cares about it and chooses to be present with us as we try to cope with the mess we sometimes make of it.

It is interesting to note that this 'Thought' flags up some of the issues which would continue to have energy through until 2011, particularly the warning about credit and the financial winds of the City of London. But I was not claiming that political judgement was easy and shortly before the end of the Thatcher era in 1990 I delivered a 'Thought' which probed the difficulty for Church or state in drawing the line between political policies and between private and public morality.

DRAWING THE LINE, 10 JULY 1990

Yesterday it was reported that an all party Select Committee has discovered an error in previous government figures regarding the poorest 10 per cent of our population. The figures are quite technical but the outcome is that, whereas it has been previously thought that the living standards of the poorest group had been rising throughout the 1980s at a rate higher than the national average, it is now clear that their living standards have been improved by a rate well under half the national rate. The gap between rich and poor is widening.

The previous figures had been used as evidence by those who believe in the trickle-down theory of wealth, the theory that if the richest members of society increase their wealth, it trickles down, and eventually everybody, even the poorest, benefit. The corrected figures seem to puncture this theory. It now seems that there are sizable pockets of poverty in our society which are impervious to the trickle down of wealth. This should surprise nobody, least of all those of us who've been working with those in the more battered parts of our nation and in recent years all political parties have suggested legislation which better targets the poor and vulnerable.

It's 50 years since Winston Churchill became prime minister. He once said, 'We want to draw a line below which we will not allow persons to live and labour, yet above which they may compete with all the strength of their manhood. We want to have free competition upwards. We decline to allow free competition to run downwards.' Well it's no easy matter to draw the line between free competition and social care and we should wish the all party Select Committee well as they struggle with the consequences of their latest figures.

The Church also has difficulty in knowing where to draw the line. But for us it's the line between private and public morality. The line between charitable giving and campaigning for social change. This dilemma is particularly acute for aid agencies like Oxfam and Christian Aid who are tackling problems of deprivation on a global scale, where it is blindingly obvious that Western wealth does not trickle down unaided and where the pockets of deprivation are thousands of square miles in scale.

Where to draw the line, for there's need for the Church to avoid the danger of concentrating solely upon personal or individual salvation to the neglect of the common good, but also there's the danger of the Church becoming so enmeshed in political and public matters that it loses the sharpness of the Christian story which brings new hope to the community and the individual. We need a theology both of poverty and of plenty, a theology rooted in the economics of sharing, whilst giving primacy to face-to-face love as the basis of friendship and community life. It's that kind of a theology, I believe, which is at the heart of the Bible's teaching.

In theory a 'Thought' on the BBC should be balanced and certainly not favour any particular party political position. It is of course not easy to be balanced in a script, strictly under three minutes long, but every now and then I risked mentioning the politics of a particular party. Here are two 'Thoughts' presented after the party concerned had lost a general election. The first follows the Conservative party defeat in 1997 heralding in the government of New Labour with Tony Blair as prime minister. It is a reminder that politics is not just about politics; human beings with their thoughts and emotions get caught up into the grindings of the political machine.

THE TORY PARTY IN BEREAVEMENT, 7 MAY 1997

Ministers of religion see a great deal of the shadow side of life. In particular the aftermath of death – bereavement, the shock, the disbelief, the denial which often follows even a long expected calamity. In the middle of the night last Friday, as the general election results began to appear I saw all those emotions on the faces of many of the defeated candidates, and their grief was only too public as it was captured on television screens around the country. Nor I suspect has the pain of loss yet diminished, for even those returning to Parliament are grieving the loss of familiar colleagues and a familiar way of life in government. The Tory party is in bereavement.

What do we normally say to people following a death. We say: don't wallow in blame – criticizing yourself and others for things you may or may not have done better – it doesn't help and harsh words said now may cause permanent rifts in the family We say: don't be greedy and squabble over the inheritance – if you do, it will turn to dust and ashes in your hands. We say: don't take any important decisions – give yourself time to grieve your loss, and honour the past before making any serious plans for the future; for now you're not thinking clearly – your heart is in shock and your mind is clouded.

What goes for individuals goes for political parties. Our democracy depends upon a healthy government and a healthy loyal opposition. It's in the interests of us all for the Tory party to come out of its time of grief in as healthy a state as possible. So I hope it doesn't wallow in blame, tearing itself apart in mutual recrimination – that would be a luxury the country can't afford. I hope that naked personal ambition isn't too obvious as the survivors pick over the inheritance. It's not too inspiring. And because people in shock don't often make wise decisions I hope that the party will give itself ample time before choosing a new leader.

All human life is in the Bible. The people of Israel when they were going through a bad patch chose a leader in haste – Saul. They soon regretted it. He looked good leadership material but he turned out to have severe character flaws. He was a disaster and it took them decades to get rid of him. Be warned.

Bishop John Taylor, referring to bereavement, once wrote, 'Almighty God, give us we pray the faithfulness to endure the dark uncertainty.' That is true wisdom. To endure such a time of dark uncertainty is surely, in life or politics, far better than making impetuous decisions.

The second 'Thought' on the subject follows the crushing defeat of the Labour government by then led by Gordon Brown who resigned shortly afterwards. The struggle to be leader of the party was fierce, made all the more dramatic by two brothers – David and Ed Miliband – being two of the candidates. It has been said that all human life is to be found in the pages of the Bible. It certainly seemed to me that the filial struggle between the Miliband brothers had been foreshadowed centuries ago in the equally fierce struggle for the birthright between the brothers Jacob and Esau.

JACOB AND ESAU, 28 SEPTEMBER 2010

There's a biblical saga which has echoes of some recent news events. It's the story of two brothers, Jacob and Esau. The younger brother Jacob persuaded his father, near death, to bestow the elder son's blessing on him When Esau later came to his father he was distraught to discover that his birthright had been stolen from him by his brother and he swore revenge. Jacob fled, hoping that time and distance might do their healing work. In the event both brothers prospered materially, but nevertheless Jacob was very anxious some years later when he heard that Esau was approaching him with a large force. He went to his brother and offered to give him a large number of sheep, goats and camels but the peace offering wasn't necessary for the elder brother ran up to the younger, threw his arms around his neck and kissed him and they both wept tears of reconciliation.

It was difficult not to be reminded of that, oh so human, story when the picture of David Miliband embracing his younger brother was shown on our TV screens. This was no stealing of a birthright blessing, for Ed's triumph had come through an open and fair election. Nevertheless, with it long being taken for granted by many party members that the mantle of leadership would eventually fall on the elder brother, his disappointment must have been hard to take. In the biblical story both brothers prospered and any bitterness or resentment was put behind them. The first signs are that the same will be true for the Miliband brothers but clearly there are important decisions David has yet to announce which will affect not only his brother but his party.

But there's more to the biblical story than the human tale of personal triumph, revenge and reconciliation, for Jacob and Esau were to become the founders of two great nations, Israel and Edom, and their later histories would reflect the founding story of birthright disputes and lesser blessings, with the people of Israel struggling to hold onto the land which they believed had been given in blessing to their forefather Jacob and the surrounding peoples often living with a sense of resentment that they had lost some of their rightful land.

And of course this is no mere historical saga: it's very much part of the story which forms the present dispute concerning Israeli settlements around Jerusalem and the West Bank. Jacob and Esau found it in them to embrace and weep tears of forgiveness; it might be a little too much to hope that outcome for the present talks between Israel and the Palestinians, but some reconciliation and mutual understanding is necessary if both states are to prosper. Surely both peoples deserve better than permanent hostility.

Britain experienced five prime ministers, all very different in personality and politics, in the period covered by these 'Thoughts': Margaret Thatcher, John Major, Tony Blair, Gordon Brown and David Cameron. Meanwhile the world outside Britain was not keeping still. In particular, against all predictions, the world saw the collapse of communism in the Soviet bloc and the end of apartheid in South Africa. Both communism and apartheid had seemed so impregnable, both backed up by military might, that it had seemed inconceivable that they would not continue into a new millennium.

The 'Thought' 'Keeping My Head Down' was delivered in July 1989 at the cusp of the collapse of communism in Eastern Europe. President George Bush (Sr) had addressed the Polish parliament the previous day, and the Berlin Wall was to be demolished four months later.

KEEPING MY HEAD DOWN, 11 JULY 1989

Mr Kruschev, the then general secretary of the communist party in the Soviet Union, was once addressing a gathering of party officials. After his talk a voice called out from the back, 'What were you doing when Stalin was carrying out his purges?' Kruschev said, 'Will the person who asked that question please stand up and then I'll answer him?' Nobody moved. 'Yes,' said Kruschev, 'and that's exactly what I was doing – keeping my head down.'

President Bush yesterday addressed the Polish parliament in Warsaw. He promised them $100 million to give a boost to Polish businesses. They wished him the long life of a hundred years. The remarkable developments during the last few years in Poland, through the efforts of members of the Church and of the Solidarity Movement are a reminder to us that people don't always keep their heads down even in difficult and dangerous times and when they have the courage to speak out, occasionally they trigger off an avalanche of public opinion. Few of us have that sort of courage, but even the most cautious of us have moments when we feel that we have to witness to our deepest hopes and dreams.

Some 20 years ago I was teaching electronics in the Engineering Department of the University of Zambia. As a priest, I also acted as chaplain and was on the staff of the cathedral. The Zambian government had entered into technical agreements with several nations and our staff in the department included three British, two Americans, and six academics from the Soviet Union. As colleagues we worked together well enough but this was still in the days of the Cold War, and it was obvious that each of the lecturers from the Soviet Union had been hand-picked as being ideologically sound.

Christmas came around, a working day at the university, but I was also conducting midnight communion in the cathedral. As I gave the worshippers their communion I suddenly found myself offering the chalice to one of my Russian colleagues. His eyes gazed into mine and we shared a glance of fear and wonder before I passed on to the next worshipper. There's no doubt that in those dark days, if the party had known of his presence in the cathedral that night he would have been flown back home on the next plane and never been allowed out again. What was it in the faith of that man which had caused him to risk career and safety in an act of public commitment even if it were to be known only to himself and God?

Thankfully we now live in more hopeful times, but I often reflect upon that brief incident. My colleague was no great hero, but he plucked up enough courage to make a small public act which reminded him of what he truly believed. Such small acts create the climate which enables the heroic acts to be effective. Let's neither despise nor underrate them. Following conscience is often a lot better than following crowds. It's not always a good idea to keep your head down.

The theme of this 'Thought' was a reminder of the difficulties that people in the Soviet Union had had during the reign of communism and the Cold War. Zambia, as a non-aligned country, was one of the few places on earth where professional people from West, East, North and South, could meet and work together as colleagues, sometimes with interesting results. From my Soviet colleagues in Zambia I learned a great deal about how individuals compromise to survive in a constant climate of fear, and how the Church survived with its faith intact until better days arrived and the faith could flourish anew.

The workshop for my political education was the newly independent country of Zambia in Central Africa. New political realities came my way there. The students at the university had marched to the French embassy protesting about an arms deal the French government had made with the apartheid regime in South Africa. The Zambian government would have agreed with the sentiments of the students but the students had not gone to the trouble of getting the right authorization for the march. There was a clash with the police and the university was closed. The Minister of Home Affairs, thinking that expatriate university lecturers must have been behind the trouble, served deportation notices on the two most popular. The rest of us were outraged and demanded a meeting with the minister. The president, Kenneth Kaunda, had been away whilst all this was going on but he graciously agreed to meet with us. We met in a lecture theatre at the university and the president listened carefully to our complaints and promised that he would investigate and correct any mistakes that might have been made. Unknown to us until later, whilst the president had been talking to us, the expatriate staff were being put on the plane to London. The deportations stood. On reflection I realized that the realities of political power in Zambia, certainly at that time, meant that a president soon came to a decision that if he had to choose between upsetting a couple of hundred expatriate university staff or his Minister of Home Affairs, leader of a major tribe, the minister was going to win every time. Political realities are not so different at Westminster as I was later to learn.

When I presented my 'Thought' of July 1989 marking the destruction of communism in Eastern Europe, I had little idea that the other ideological bastion, apartheid, would also begin to crack that year. Economic sanctions and other pressures both outside and inside South Africa had had their effect. The Churches had been thoroughly involved in the struggle – indeed Archbishop Desmond Tutu was later to say, 'It was the Eucharist which broke apartheid.' P. W. Botha, nicknamed 'The big crocodile', in July 1989 was succeeded as South African president by F. W. de Klerk, who has generally been credited with engineering the end of apartheid. In 1990 the ban on the ANC was lifted and Nelson Mandela was released from prison. It would have been inconceivable even ten years earlier to imagine that a Nationalist President and an ANC leader who had been serving a lifelong prison sentence would jointly receive a Nobel Peace Prize, but in 1993 F. W. de Klerk and Nelson Mandela stepped up to the podium together to jointly receive the honour. It had been well deserved, for the two leaders were working closely together in seeking to take the country to a new future without violence.

I had first-hand experience of that partnership at work. Before Nelson Mandela's release from prison, for over a decade I had been chairman of a British charity called 'The Luthuli Trust'. It had been set up to help educate at Western universities the children of those caught up in the struggle against apartheid in South Africa. The work involved raising money for the airfares, university fees, living expenses and so on. Over the years, and with the aid of money raised in Britain and Europe, several hundred students had graduated successfully in a variety of subjects. Shortly after Nelson Mandela's release from prison, the money for the trust dried up. Perhaps understandably the donors felt that this work outside South Africa was no longer needed and they directed their funds to the educational needs within the country. We still had almost 200 students studying, however, and we had no funds to enable them to complete their studies and return home.

I sought an appointment with the South African High Commissioner in London, a white politician from the Nationalist party, which was still in power. I said, 'This is the first time I have been in this building. I am more used to picketing it from outside.' He replied, 'We live in changing times.' I explained that my trust needed up to £200,000 in order for his fellow citizens to finish their studies and return home to help in nation building. He told me that he did not have the authority to donate such a large sum of money, but if I were to get the signature of Nelson Mandela on a letter of request, anything was possible. My ANC contacts set up a meeting with their president. I went to his office in Johannesburg at 8 o'clock in the morning and said to his secretary that it was good of the president to see me so early. 'This isn't early,' she said, 'he's at his desk at 6 o'clock every morning. He's got a lot of time to make up.' It was said of President Lincoln that he had a small motor inside him which never rested, and the same is surely true of Nelson Mandela. Carefully and meticulously he considered my request and I flew back to London with the necessary letter. The High Commissioner was as good as his word and we received the funds. Such cooperation between Nationalist and ANC leaders and officials oiled the wheels of a smooth transition of power in 1994.

In all the years of imprisonment Nelson Mandela never gave up hope; the motor inside him never ceased planning for the future. In 1994 he was able to start putting those plans into action. My 'Thought' of 29 April 1994 marked the day that the South African people, with a new race-free constitution, went to the polls.

THE KEYS TO THE FUTURE OF SOUTH AFRICA, 29 APRIL 1994

When we lived in Zambia in Central Africa a few years after independence we witnessed a general election. Democracy in that country was still new and people were still excited about casting their vote. One prospective MP campaigned waving a large key – his message was simple: 'This is the key of parliament – if you don't vote for me, nobody will be able to get in.'

Today the people of South Africa are virtually certain to give the key of parliament to Nelson Mandela. For 27 years he was behind lock and key but now he will have the task of building a nation where deep and abiding tribal loyalties must find their place within the unity of a modern state.

St Paul might have been able to give him a little advice. Faith, hope and charity were to be the building blocks of the new Christian Church and they could be equally important foundations of the new South Africa. First the new government will need faith. It will need to keep the faith of the white tribes if their experience and wealth are not to bleed away. But just as important, the new government will need to keep faith with the black tribes. More than a generation of South Africans have lost out on schooling, housing and jobs. They have braved violence and terror to cast their vote – woe betide the government if it fails to keep faith with them.

Secondly, the new government will need hope and there is much to be hopeful about. South Africa has tremendous resources – natural and human. It could be the powerhouse of Africa. When Zambia achieved independence it had just six black Zambian graduates. South Africa has hundreds of black graduates who either qualified in their own country before the education system was ruined for such people, or as refugees have studied or worked in responsible positions outside their home country. South Africa has no shortage of trained talent, black or white; put that alongside the natural wealth of the country and the energy of its peoples and there is reason for hope.

Provided St Paul's third virtue is also present – charity. The country comes to majority rule after decades of pain and struggle. Many people bear many wounds – they have been provoked beyond endurance, and yet through the grace of God and through the recent partnership of Mandela and De Klerk the country has not exploded in violence. If the country is to go forward in unity there now has to be charity in abundance – forgiveness for past wrongs, patience when future hopes fail to materialize sufficiently swiftly.

Nelson Mandela today will be handed the keys of parliament, but the keys of nation building are even more important – the keys of faith, hope and charity – and the greatest of these is charity.

The hard work of nation building had begun but the risks of disaster were very real. Many people had been damaged during the oppressive regime of apartheid and many wanted the perpetrators to be punished. Nelson Mandela, who had spent his first night of freedom at Archbishop's House in Cape Town, asked Archbishop Desmond Tutu to chair the 'Truth and Reconciliation Commission' persuading the nation to take a different course, which whilst thoroughly examining past wrongs did not allow them to poison nation building in the future. This is surely one of the best examples in our times of the Church as the transformer of the state – being thoroughly involved in the life of the nation but bringing something distinctive from its own faith perspective.

Of course nation building in Africa and elsewhere in developing countries depends much upon factors beyond their own control and in particular, conditions of world trade. Christians and the Churches had always given generously to aid development through agencies such as Christian Aid but toward the end of the century it was becoming increasingly clear that trade, not aid, was the key to development, and Church groups became thoroughly involved in the campaigns for trade justice. This was the topic on my 'Thought' in July 2004. There was reason for hope. In Britain both the prime minister and Chancellor of the Exchequer were sympathetic to increasing the aid budget provided the public were behind it and the 'Make Poverty History' campaign was mobilizing a great deal of popular support and was focusing its attention at the G8 summit to be held in Britain in 2005. It was hoped that this would build on the success of the Jubilee 2000 campaign which had been very influential in a previous meeting of the G8 in Birmingham in 1998

TRADE JUSTICE, 13 July 2004

There'll be some 100,000 civil servants this morning who won't be too pleased with yesterday's financial statement from the Chancellor of the Exchequer because their jobs are due to disappear. But I'm delighted at another piece of his news – the intention to increase the Aid budget by over 9 per cent. It's needed.

Aid is one weapon in the fight against world poverty; another is trade. Therefore the White Paper which was published by the Department of Trade and Industry last week may prove to be just as significant as the Chancellor's aid news, for the paper revisits the UK's approach to world trade, particularly where it impacts upon developing countries.

The White Paper argues for flexibility in world trade – the one size fits all approach doesn't work. It is indeed paradoxical that Western countries have used the logic of free trade to press developing countries to open up their markets while at the same time adopting protectionist measures at home. The effect has been to virtually destroy the livelihood of producers in many developing countries as cheap food from the West floods in and distorts local prices.

The White Paper calls for a system that allows developing countries to remove trade barriers at a pace and in a way that lies within their own development plans. This would be some u-turn in current international economic thought and would see an end to the pernicious practice of the IMF and the World Bank threatening developing nations with swinging financial cuts if they don't remove trade barriers which protect their farmers.

And perhaps the DTI would go a further step and work to remove those trade barriers in Europe which keep out goods manufactured in the developing world. Let me tell you about Divine chocolate. It's heavenly chocolate with a bitter edge. It's manufactured and marketed by Christian Aid to support cocoa bean farmers in Africa. Christian Aid would prefer them to make the chocolate too, but it's not possible. There's a mere 3 per cent tariff on cocoa beans coming into Europe, but chocolate coming in would attract a 30 per cent tariff. So Christian Aid does the best it can. It imports the cocoa beans and manufactures the chocolate in Germany. African farmers get the benefit of the price of fairly traded beans but can't add the value that manufactured goods would bring. How can local businesses begin to flourish with that sort of a handicap?

There's a new moral energy around the issue of trade justice and in 2005, with Britain president both of the EU and the G8 summit, there's a sense that we're at a tipping point. I've heard Christian hope defined as believing despite the evidence, and then seeing the evidence change. We might well see the evidence change in 2005. Jesus in the Sermon on the Mount said, 'Give, and it will be given to you, a good measure, pressed down, running over. For with the measure you use, it will be measured to you.' That would be no bad starting point for trade justice for rich and poor alike. God gives freely, generously, abundantly; there's no reason for us not to do likewise.

Hopes were high then that the mobilization of so many people – Christians, Churches and Church groups amongst them – would make a real difference at the coming G8 summit at Gleneagles in July 2005. We were seeing another way in which the Church can act as a transformer of political life. In the event, sadly, on the morning of the first full day of the G8 summit, as we have discussed in the last chapter, suicide bombers blew up several trains on the London Underground. This obviously dominated the news, and Tony Blair, the prime minister, had to temporarily leave the summit for London. With the world a few years later to face an unprecedented financial collapse we had seen the high-water mark of the 'Make Poverty History' campaign; we were back to the hard work of seeking to win the argument step by step in hard financial times. There were to be other hopeful signs, however, like Gordon Brown, then prime minister and himself a son of the manse, leading all the bishops attending the Lambeth Conference in 2008 on a 'Walk of Witness' down Whitehall, and then giving a speech encouraging Church leaders in all countries to keep the pressure on their governments to work to meet the Millennium Development Goals.

The mobilization of ordinary Church folk in order to transform political life for the common good was seen in another guise in the United States. Conservative evangelical Churches, particularly in the South, had always used their political muscle, and several presidents, seeking their votes, had declared themselves 'born again' Christians. Mainline Churches of a more liberal persuasion began to follow their example, particularly in local politics. The philosophy behind this is that if you want to change political life you must be able to deliver money or people. Churches are not able to generate large sums of money and neither should they, but they can mobilize people if they organize themselves. I pointed to this in January 2009 when a new US president, Barack Obama, with a background in community politics, was about to take office.

DON'T THEY KNOW THE ELECTION'S OVER? 14 JANUARY 2009

We are in the last days of an American presidency for which special relationships around the globe have been very important. I'm rather hoping that the new president, with his background in local community organizing will have a different emphasis, for special relationships can get us all into a lot of trouble.

Some years ago I spent some time in New York and my host was a local church minister very much involved in community organizing. He shared with me some basic principles. 'If you really want to change things,' he said, 'you must be prepared to work with others who must be able to deliver either finance or people. Without either of those, vision is just talk. Politicians can deliver finance; faith communities can deliver people.'

He told the story of the candidate for mayor of New York. It seems that he came and spoke to a gathering of concerned citizen from New York churches. He promised that if he was successful in the election he would return and listen carefully to their concerns. He was successful and a return visit was organized. It was agreed that the new mayor wouldn't speak. He'd simply listen to what the churches wished to tell him about their community fears, hopes and plans. They prepared carefully for the meeting. The evening came and the mayor arrived. As he strode onto the platform he told the chair, 'I've changed my mind. I will listen to what your people have to say, but first I want to give them a twenty-minute speech about my own plans for the city.'

'That wasn't the contract,' said the chair. 'Well,' said the mayor, 'that's the way it is, and if I can't do it my way, I'm off.' And so saying he strode out. As he reached the door he said in irritation to one of his aides, 'Don't these guys realize that the election is over.' Unfortunately, for him, the aside was overheard and was in the news the next morning.

The following Saturday the churches brought several thousand people to stand silently outside city hall. Within a fortnight the mayor was back at the Church community meeting, and this time the contract was kept and he did listen. It was the start of a different sort of relationship between people of faith and local politicians. A relationship of respect.

Well, the presidential election is over in America, and we live in challenging times where none of us have clear answers, but I think that we're learning that although special relationships can be useful because they build on common views and values, they can blind our vision and distort our judgement. It was only when the early Church began to listen to the outsiders – the gentiles, the slaves, the women – and involve them in the common task, that the vision of a new world took off, and what's true of faith may well be true of politics.

Reinhold Niebuhr, the elder brother of Richard mentioned earlier in the chapter, once wrote, 'Human sinfulness makes democracy necessary and human goodness makes it possible.' Religion brings knowledge of both human sinfulness and goodness to the political table. By staying clear sighted about both, the Church can act as a transformer of political life. When it does, the common life is enriched. As related in previous chapters this theory has been severely tested in recent times by a series of overseas wars in which Britain has been involved and by terrorism on the British mainland but these have not been the sole situations which have raised ethical questions which the nation and its leaders have had to face. The following chapter will address some of these.

4

Religion and Public Ethics

The areas of life for which people most look to religion for guidance are those of personal morality and public ethics. They are related but are not the same. The golden rule of personal morality common to most religions is to love your neighbour as yourself but the young lawyer in the gospel story was then quick to ask Jesus, 'But who is my neighbour?' In answering that question we move from the love of the neighbour in front of us to the care also of the neighbour distant from us in space and time. We move from personal morality to public ethics. A story told by Lord Tonypandy rather helpfully illustrates this. I recalled it in a 'Thought' given shortly after his death in September 1997

WHAT'S ETHICS, 24 SEPTEMBER 1997

I was sorry to hear of the death of George Thomas, Lord Tonypandy, the previous speaker of the House of Commons. He was a great public servant, a lovely man with a fund of entertaining stories. I remember him relating how, as a boy, he had heard someone use the word 'ethics', and not knowing what it meant, he went to ask his father who kept a drapers' shop. 'Dad, what's ethics?' There was a thoughtful silence and then his father replied. 'Well son, suppose a customer came into the shop and made a purchase with a five pound note, thinking that it was a one pound note; ethics is, do I tell my partner about it?'

Well, I once heard a lecture given on business ethics. It was very short, consisting of three words: 'There aren't any'. That, I think, is overcynical; after all, the visitor to every business or organization today is met with a prominent 'Mission Statement', full of high-minded phrases about customer satisfaction and ethical standards, but in our competitive

world of competing global economies does that in practice add up to
more than the customer getting a free bag of crisps if she or he spends
more than £30 at the checkout.

No, when it comes to business ethics, I actually think that Lord
Tonypandy's dad was onto something – 'Do I tell my partner about it.'
– because ethics I believe consists of taking our network of obligations
seriously. In the competitive 1980s we were encouraged just to look after
ourselves and our nearest and dearest. If everybody did that, the theory
went, the world would be no bad place. This I fear flew in the face of
centuries of religious experience that when everybody acts selfishly, the
world goes to hell. But neither is every businesswoman cut out to be a
Mother Teresa, and the shareholders wouldn't like it if she were. In the
caring 1990s we have to find the way of balancing our responsibilities
to our nearest and dearest, and our nearest neighbour, with our wider
responsibilities to our distant neighbour including future generations.

Lord Tonypandy's dad had such a network of responsibilities. He had
a responsibility to himself, the pride and satisfaction of building up a
decent business; to his wife and family to provide them with the means
for a decent life and education, particularly if any of them were to have a
chance of becoming speaker of the House of Commons. He had a respon-
sibility to his partner if the partnership were to be long-standing. He had
a responsibility to the people of the town to provide a decent service at
reasonable cost; to the local Chamber of Commerce to play his part in
building up the prosperity of the town; to pay his taxes to help provide
public service and support for less fortunate families. It was a wide net.

Yes. And he also had a responsibility to the customer, and on reflection
I bet he called him back, and said, 'Mr Jones – I think you've made a
mistake.'

If ethics is our way of acting well in the network of responsibilities we
all have, public ethics is based and regulated by the rule of law which
itself has the desire for justice at its heart. It might be said that love
between individuals becomes, in wider terms, justice between groups

and nations. In Christian traditional teaching human laws lie at the base of a hierarchy of law. Overarching all is Divine Law – the will of God for creation stemming out of his own nature of justice and grace. How are human beings to know the requirements of Divine Law? In two ways: first, there is Natural Law, discerned by the reflection of rational men and women in the created order. Because God was the Creator, the creation, it is argued, bears his imprint and nature, so the study of the laws of nature is a powerful way of understanding something of Divine Law. This way of thinking perhaps helps us understand why the discipline of science was developed most fully in Western societies built on Christian foundations.

But Christianity is not a panentheistic religion. The teaching is that, whilst God created his creation and continues to breathe life into it, God and nature are not identical. God remains transcendent and separate from his creation and so his nature cannot be totally discerned through the study of nature, however meticulously it is conducted. There is a further element to Divine Law then, which cannot be uncovered by human probing – it must be revealed by God. So it is called Revealed Law and it is revealed most clearly through the biblical record and the life of Jesus Christ. Through the study of Natural Law and Revealed Law together, the nature of Divine Law is available to the human mind, and human laws, devised to serve the common good, should be drawn from it.

In recent years the law lords have moved out of the House of Lords and this is clearly symbolic of the separation of judges from Parliament. It is the role of Parliament to frame laws and of the judiciary to interpret them. With the incorporation of European Human Rights legislation into British law, judges are making rulings which are sometimes very uncomfortable for government ministers whatever their politics. We had a first hint of this in 2005 as is seen in my 'Thought' given in the August of that year.

RULE OF LAW, 12 AUGUST 2005

Ten foreign nationals were taken into custody yesterday preparatory to deportation because the Home secretary believes that under present circumstances they pose a threat to national security. To quote the prime minister, 'The rules are changing.' Of course this doesn't mean that they'll be flying out today or tomorrow, for no doubt there'll be a long process of appeal before the courts.

There are two fundamental principles of the British constitution: one is the sovereignty of Parliament; the other is the rule of law. This separation of powers has served us well over the years and has been much admired around the globe, but the recent incorporation of European Human Rights legislation into British law has blurred the edges. People warned when Parliament was first debating this that if we weren't very careful we would get judge-made law. As legislation in a dozen or more bills covering employment rights, law and order matters, education, and civil partnerships came before Parliament, ministers were asked to spell out on the face of the bill what precisely was being proposed, and again and again the answer was, in the words of the previous Lord Chancellor, 'Let the courts decide.' In other words we will only get clarity about what human rights legislation means in Britain when case after case has gone before the courts and case law has gradually been built up.

This is dangerous because it almost sets up a process where quite frequently courts and judges will seem to be challenging the desires of government. But it's also dangerous because law is far too important just to be left to the judges and the politicians, and if we allow government and the courts to be permanently at odds our national life will be weakened.

And with faith matters being at the heart of present disputes its well to be reminded that in the seventeenth century, when the British consti-tution was still being formed, one of the great Anglican scholars, Richard Hooker, argued that because even God works according to the law of his own divine nature, people of faith – Anglican, Puritan, Catholic, in those days; today Christian, Muslim, Hindu, Sikh, Jew – mustn't think it a matter of indifference either to yield or not to yield obedience to law.

Right law is for the common good of us all. It's not just a matter of whether or not we run the risk of containing people here who might pose a risk to our security or force them to take the risk of possible torture or death in countries to which they might be sent. More significantly, in a democratic society, people of faith, for reasons of faith, have a duty to help form the laws of the land, and then live by them.

Another important contribution Christian tradition can make to the public understanding of the nature of right law is the Christian balance between law and grace. Law is necessary because free people must be prepared to have limits on their personal freedom for the common good. Grace is necessary because in such a world mistakes are made and individuals and society need the grace of God to give them the strength to pick up their lives and move on. This has practical consequences in the way society treats those who offend against the law.

Diocesan bishops tend to take a great interest in the prisons in their diocese. Bishops are privileged in having instant access to any prison in their diocese and they have the right to go anywhere within those prisons. Many bishops use this privilege to inform themselves about the way in which prisons work and so remove some of the common myths and misrepresentation. There are very few votes to be collected in favour of prison reform and few politicians have it as one of their main concerns. With their first-hand knowledge this is an area where bishops can make a real contribution both in Parliament and in seeking to inform public opinion.

One of the scandals in the present system is the way in which offenders return to prison again and again. Obviously there must be an element of punishment in a prison sentence to express society's disapproval on the act of law-breaking, but society is in no way protected if an offender returns to prison soon after his release. Rehabilitation as much as punishment is in the interest of both the offender and society. This is not always given the highest priority in the prison system. I came upon an example of that fact in another of my prison visits.

Food is a sensitive matter in any institution, and a prison is no exception. When much of your life is governed for you and becomes a matter of grinding routine, the menu is virtually the only point of decision making during the day. In a prison, a disappointing choice can lead to a nasty incident. And because the work is popular, the kitchen is always a hive of activity. I always made a point, therefore, in my quite frequent visits to prisons, of spending some time in the kitchen.

I was rather surprised on one such visit to find that all was calm and orderly. I asked the officer in charge what had happened. 'It's wonderful,' he said, 'I now control my own budget.' 'What difference does that make?' I asked. 'Oh, I now don't employ any prisoners; I can't afford them.' 'What do you mean,' I said, 'surely prison labour is cheap?' 'No it's not,' came the answer. 'Prisoners are unskilled. They break things, and they don't have work discipline. It's much more efficient to bring in skilled labour from outside.' 'Yes,' I argued, 'but surely kitchen work was very popular with prisoners as a way of learning new skills?' 'That's not my area of concern bishop,' the good man replied. 'That's a matter for the governor.' So for seemingly sensible and economic reasons, prisoners who previously would, no doubt in clumsy ways, have gained work experience in the kitchens were now banged up in their cells and came out without skill, ready to go back to thieving.

I am please to read that the recently appointed Minister of Justice, Kenneth Clarke, is not only asking questions about the rehabilitation element in a prison sentence, but also whether prison sentences themselves are always in the public interest. I hope he will survive, for such questions are not always welcome either in the media or in Parliament. A 'Thought' given in June 2008 raised the question of restorative justice as an alternative to a prison sentence.

RESTORATIVE JUSTICE, 17 JUNE 2008

Proposals due to be published this week reviews ways of tackling crime and punishment. If the reports are true the recommendations are quite dramatic. They attempt to restore the public's confidence in the justice system by introducing tougher and more visible punishments. So, for example, offenders sentenced to community punishment would be put to work wearing high visibility bibs to identify them as criminals. This would be very noticeable for at present tens of thousands of offenders carry out unpaid community payback work. Would it help to tackle crime and make the streets safer if such people were shamed in this modernized version of the chain gang? For some, perhaps it would, for to avoid such humiliation they might well prefer to avoid a life of crime. For others, lack of self-esteem is already at the heart of their antisocial behaviour, and shaming them so publically might well alienate them further from the wider community.

Traditionally the Church has thought of love and justice as the poles between which human interaction must move. Justice punishes, love heals. Between these poles there is a process of accountability in which shaming and repentance might well have a part to play before community and victim are ready to forgive and the perpetrator is ready and able to make a fresh start. Harsh visible punishments might seem to be appropriate and just, but those most closely involved in working with young offenders are discovering that it is when offenders are brought face to face with their victims, and forced to recognize over a period of time the human consequences of their actions, that true repentance happens and life changes can occur.

This doesn't happen easily, and neither are we just talking about the offender and the victim. Many more people are involved and affected by every crime. The offender has a family and social network which is often critical to their behaviour. The victim's family and social network equally might have been fractured. And the fabric of the local community is weakened by any crime and so wider society has an interest in ensuring that a balanced justice is achieved in which the needs of victims are fully

*attended to, offenders are made actively responsible for their actions,
and the punishment leads to a reintegration of both into the community.*

*High-visibility brightly coloured bibs might have a part to play in this,
but it is the low visibility conversation between offender and victim,
enabled and organized by skilled community personnel, which brings
the real changes. And it's a costly business – financially and emotionally.*

If the return again and again of petty offenders to prison to serve short
sentences is wasteful in terms of human lives and financial resources,
a different question is raised with the most serious offenders serving
mandatory life sentences.

I was once at an unusual conference which took place inside the
walls of a Category A prison. The audience consisted almost entirely of
prisoners serving a mandatory life sentence for murder. Of course very
few prisoners actually serve a life sentence because the trial judge sets a
tariff – the number of years that the prisoner must serve before he or she
can be considered for parole. The speaker was an ex-prisoner who had
been released on parole a couple of years earlier. He said, 'I don't know
why you're all getting so excited about the length of your tariff; mine was
nine years, but the parole board made me serve 25.'

This brought home to me the fact that the tariff is simply part of the
process, and that no prisoner is released on parole unless he or she is
considered to be of no danger to the community and even then he or she
can be recalled at any time for the life-sentence still stands. Sometimes
there are very hard cases, none more so than Myra Hindley whose case I
addressed in a 'Thought' in 1997. She had begun her life sentence in 1966
following her conviction for her part in the murder of children and their
burial on Saddleworth Moor.

MYRA HINDLEY ET. AL, 27 MAY 1997

*The trial of the two nurses accused of murdering their colleague in Saudi
Arabia has been adjourned whilst the victim's relations are consulted
as to whether they wish the death penalty to be inflicted should the*

court find the accused guilty. The trial judge announced that this was a wonderful opportunity to display how Islamic justice can bring reconciliation between wronged parties. That might be so, but it leaves me deeply disturbed because the immediate effect seems to be to force the two accused to plead for mercy when in fact they haven't yet been found guilty of any crime.

The fundamental difference between this venerable system of justice and our own is that with the Islamic system the penalty for the crime is partly determined by the victims, whereas in our system the penalty, within the limits set by Parliament, is decided by the trial judge. This should ensure consistent treatment and parity of punishment.

Occasionally we seem to fall between the two systems. I regularly visit a prison in Leicestershire where all the prisoners are on a mandatory life sentence. In many cases the trial judge will have recommended a minimum tariff. In some horrific crimes this will be the natural lifespan of the person, but in most cases it will be the minimum number of years which must be served before parole can even be considered by the Home Secretary. This at least gives the prisoner something to hope for, and gives the prison authorities a base to begin the process of rehabilitation.

The Home Secretary, in making his decision over parole, considers many factors including public opinion, and here we being to edge towards the Islamic system, because public opinion is after all the opinion of victims writ large and the victim's view of the crime is likely to be harsher than that of a dispassionate trial judge. We have the classic case of Myra Hindley who has already served far longer than the tariff set by the trial judge who in her case deliberately set a minimum period of years of imprisonment whilst recommending natural life for her accomplice. It would seem that public opinion disagrees with the learned judge.

This might be right, but again it leaves me feeling uneasy. In the Saudi Arabian case we see the complications which can arise when victims overinfluence punishment. Do we really want to see that here? Our system is built on the twin Christian virtues of justice and mercy, loving the sinner whilst hating the sin. I believe that a trial judge is best able to balance these two principles and so produce a sentence reflecting the seriousness of the crime whilst still holding out some hope for the sinner.

Myra Hindley died in prison in November 2002.

The rule of law was to prove of supreme importance when Britain agreed to join the United States in the Invasion of Iraq in 2003. President Bush was less concerned about this, believing that regime change was legitimate in the case of an oppressive and dangerous dictator such as Saddam Hussein. This was not the British government's view and it worked hard to argue the case, both domestically and at the United Nations, for the legality of invading Iraq in order to remove the danger from any weapons of mass destruction. Eventually, after many misgivings, the Attorney General gave his advice that he believed that, in the light of earlier UN resolutions, the invasion would be legal. But much depended upon the truthfulness of the claims of informers that such WDM existed and could be mobilized. In the event the invasion revealed this claim to be untrue. These intelligence sources provided some of the ingredients in the dossier which the prime minister presented to Parliament in September 2002 which included the claim that WMD could be mobilized within 45 minutes. In May 2003 when British troops were advancing through Basra the BBC commentator Andrew Gilligan on the *Today* programme said, 'What we've been told by one of the senior officials in charge of drawing up that dossier was that actually the government probably knew that the 45-minute figure was wrong before it decided to put it in …' Downing Street went ballistic at this very damaging allegation and one of the repercussions was that Dr David Kelly, believed to be one of Gilligan's sources, took his own life. An inquiry into his death chaired by Lord Hutton, a law lord and former judge in Northern Ireland, reported at the end of January 2004. My 'Thought' presented shortly afterwards discusses the nature of public truth.

TRUTH, 2 FEBRUARY 2004

In the last chapter of the first novel about Harry Potter, the lad is strug-gling to understand what is going on. He says to Dumbledore, the kindly, shrewd headmaster, 'Sir there are some things I'd like to know, if you can tell me ... things I want to know the truth about.' 'The truth,' Dumbledore sighed, 'It is a beautiful and terrible thing, and should therefore be treated with great caution.'

I think that we've been discovering that in the last few days. The Hutton report probes the facts surrounding David Kelly's death. President Bush says that he wants to know the facts behind any intelligence failure in the run-up to war in Iraq. But uncovering the basic facts of a situation isn't necessarily the same as uncovering the truth. That can be a far more demanding task. Thomas Gradgrind in Dickens' Hard Times *might declare, 'In this life, we want nothing but Facts, sir, nothing but Facts,' but facts mishandled can obscure or even distort truth.*

When Jesus stood in chains before Pilate, the facts seemed quite straightforward to the Roman judge. A charismatic rabble-rouser had been arrested by the lawful authorities who now wanted him put to death. But all was not what it seemed. Jesus said to Pilate, 'For this was I born and came into the world, to bear witness to the truth.' To which Pilate replied, 'What is truth?' – and civically sent him to his death.

What is truth and how do we recognize it? Soon after independence in Zambia in the late 1960s there was tight censorship of radio and TV, with the news broadcasts being vetted by the president's office. There was just one uncensored news programme, because in the run-up to independence that presenter, Colin Morris, had been extremely critical of the colonialist regime and President Kaunda, said that he had earned the right to be critical of his new government if he wished. So every Sunday lunchtime he would sit on the corner of a table, look into the TV camera, and for half an hour or so give his uncensored views on the news of the week. It was riveting stuff. It had the biggest audience of any programme. Why? Because people recognized the truth when they heard it. They still do.

The Bible links truth especially with God and God's word as being firm, unchanging, reliable. There's a biblical proverb which says, 'Truthful lips endure for ever, but a lying tongue is but for a moment.' In other words, if people speak the truth then their words, like God's, will last. The test of truth is whether it stands the test of time.

This question of public truth and all the circumstances surrounding the Iraq war and its aftermath probably caused the most severe damage not only to Prime Minister Tony Blair, but perhaps to all politicians. The fact that Tony Blair was so much a conviction politician and so compelling a communicator made it all the more damaging when the public mood changed. Some people had grave doubts about whether he had been speaking truthfully when he had insisted that he believed that there were WMD in Iraq and that they were a real danger to Britain and the international community, and if he had been expressing his true beliefs at the time, whether he had allowed himself too easily to be convinced of their existence. The sense of public let-down was, I believe, one of the components of the later general undermining of respect for politicians and Parliament.

If public truth is one of the vital components of public ethics, public trust is another, and if the lack of public truth proved to be the nemesis of one British prime minister, Tony Blair, the lack of public trust proved to be gravely damaging to his successor, Gordon Brown. Nobody would have predicted that, after ten years as Chancellor of the Exchequer, it was finance which would lead to the downfall of the massively experienced new prime minister. The starting point was not lack of trust in the new prime minister – indeed at the start he was very popular – but rather lack of trust in the banking system which was at the centre of the economy and which he had presided over with confidence and pride. Within three months of his taking office, the edifice began to shake as indicated in my 'Thought' from September 2007.

TRUST AND SELFISHNESS, 18 SEPTEMBER 2007

There's a scene in the children's film Mary Poppins *when the children demand their tuppence back from their father's bank. This is resisted by the bank officials and the children get indignant. At this point all the adult customers start demanding withdrawal of their funds and before long there's a run on the bank. We've seen something like this over the weekend, when long queues have formed outside the branches of the Northern Rock Bank and over £2 billion has been withdrawn. Now in some ways this is as illogical as the Mary Poppins bank run. The Bank of England and government ministers have given assurances that there's ample money available to cover the funds of customers, but those pictures of queues make people uncertain and they get up early to join them. Of course they also know that their actions might help to cause the very crisis which frightens them, but nevertheless their trust in the bank has been shaken.*

There's something pretty fundamental going on here, for trust and altruism lie at the heart of the workings of a civilized society, and in the long run no human group can survive without these values. In the short run, however, the individual who acts selfishly in a generally trusting society will benefit; just as the law breaker in a generally law abiding society might well have short-term gains. A society generally strong and confident has the resilience to absorb a minority of antisocial behaviour, but in a shaky society in unstable times, the ripples of social breakdown can spread dangerously.

Social scientists have recently been examining such matters. One experiment takes the form of a game which tests people's altruism, selfishness and trust. In the game if everybody behaves altruistically, everybody gains, if some cheat, then they may gain initially, but everyone loses out eventually. The trouble is that in any particular exchange, you don't know whether your fellow player is cheating or not, and so your own response is likely to be formed by your own sense of trust.

What I find of interest is the overall responses of varying types of people. This isn't very good news for a Church minister like myself but it seems that the ones most trusting and altruistic tend to be those of a questioning form of spirituality, whilst firm religious believers, in this game, show up as being less generous and trusting than even the non-religious. I don't know if life mirrors the game, as Northern Rock seems to be mirroring Mary Poppins, but if it does, then those in the queue, knowing that they're being irrationally selfish but wanting to take no risks, are just as likely to be religious as not. The ones not there, the trusting ones, are those looking for a generous, trusting God – and I don't think he's to be found in bank queues.

The factor which public leaders have to come to terms with when dealing with public ethics is that the decisions which they are obliged to make are seldom obviously good or bad; the decision is to chose between what are perceived to be two desirable factors, or, more commonly, to choose, not between black or white, but between two shades of grey. Very often the public is determined to have its cake and eat it concerning some issue over which it feels strongly, or to put it another way it wants legislation which creates a circle and a square. Ministers and their senior advisers are therefore often required to attempt to square circles, and the criticism can be fierce when they fail to do so. My 'Thought' of March 2005 addressed this issue in public ethics.

SQUARING THE CIRCLE, 15 MARCH 2005

Yesterday a report from the Commons Defence Select Committee, following the still unexplained deaths of some recruits at Deepcut barracks, claimed that the army had 'failed to grasp the nettle' in its duty of care. Of course it's only a few weeks ago that we were shocked to learn of the way in which some of our soldiers in Iraq were treating civilian prisoners. We rightly demand first-class professional behaviour from our soldiery. But let's be clear about what we are asking the armed forces to do. We're asking them to take boys and girls straight from the anti-authoritarian culture of school and street, and turn them into disciplined and controlled young men and women, going against all natural instincts by being willing to risk their lives when ordered to do so. And the army has to do all that whilst having a duty of care for each one of them. It's a tall order.

Or what of some of the other stories running at the present time? On my visits to hospitals it's obvious that a great deal of money has been spent on them in recent years. Yet, yesterday the British Medical Association said that Accident and Emergency patients are being put at risk because trusts are under pressure to meet government waiting targets – a patient, it seems, to meet those targets mustn't stay in an Accident and Emergency Unit for more than four hours. The idea, of course, is that they're treated swiftly without endless delay. But after four hours, not every patient is ready to be sent home, and there aren't necessarily specialist beds ready and waiting, yet they are sometimes sent home or put on trolleys in corridors because they must leave the A and E unit if the targets are to be met. Surely the truth is that targets are good things – in health and schools they really have sharpened the minds of the professionals and upped standards. But we're back to the duty of care: some patients, some students, don't fit easily within the targets and then we're either asking our professionals to spin the figures or to neglect the individual.

Again, the chief constable of Nottingham wants more of his police officers patrolling the streets rather than filling in forms. Of course that is often said. Until, that is, a case collapses in court and some possible villain goes free because the evidence hasn't been meticulously recorded on those despised forms. One person's police officer not on the beat but wastefully back at the station filling in forms is another person's police officer making sure that the time on the beat was not wasted by making sure that the paperwork leads to a conviction.

Squaring circles is at the heart of the Christian faith. We believe God to be one and yet a Trinity of persons. We believe Jesus Christ to be both human and divine. And whenever those truths have been reduced to something more tidy and logical the new formulations have proved to be inadequate. We, the British public, are for ever asking our professionals to square circles – and that's okay, provided we suspect those who claim that it can easily be done and we don't criticize too fiercely when somebody gets it wrong.

Perhaps the most difficult circle that society and its leaders has had to attempt to square in recent decades is that of the possession of nuclear weapons. It is not only that it is questionable to set aside in times of financial cutbacks tens of billions of pounds to keep a weapon operational, when it is everybody's most fervent hope that it will never be used; it is also that since the end of the Cold War it is difficult to imagine what the international situation would be which would encourage Britain unilaterally to use its own nuclear weapons. As the following 'Thought' from August 2005 indicates, I was personally involved in these arguments when chair of the Church of England's Board of Mission and a member of delegations of the World Council of Churches to the UN when the Nuclear Non-Proliferation Treaty was being renewed every five years.

NUCLEAR WEAPONS, 5 AUGUST 2005

Sixty years ago tomorrow an atomic bomb was dropped on Hiroshima. Three weeks earlier one of its main creators, Robert Oppenheimer, watched the first test in a desert in New Mexico. He later reported that the words from the Hindu scripture, Bhagavad Gita – 'I am become death, the shatterer of worlds' – flashed through his mind when the awesome power of that first modest bomb was revealed.

Sixty years later we're still struggling with the legacy. Now there are nine nuclear nations, 27,000 nuclear bombs and getting on for 2,000 tons of plutonium. The nuclear chickens were already coming home to roost back in 1970 when the United Nations sponsored the Nuclear Non-Proliferation Treaty. It did a three-pronged deal. The nations without nuclear weapons would not seek to develop them, provided that the nations with nuclear weapons – America, Russia, France, Britain – agreed to progressively disarm; meanwhile, knowledge for the peaceful use of nuclear energy would be shared with non-nuclear nations. It was also agreed that signatories would meet at the UN every five years to review progress.

The latest review took place in May this year and I was one of the representatives of the World Council of Churches meeting with national delegations. It was a nightmare. The conference was to last a month. I arrived in week three and the delegations were still arguing about the agenda. It became pretty obvious that it was not in the interest of powerful players for the conference ever to start, for in the five years since the previous review there had been ominous developments. India and Pakistan had joined Israel in developing nuclear weapons and Korea and Iran were well on the way. Meanwhile the Americans were talking about a new generation of smart nuclear weapons and the British would soon need to decide whether or not to replace its Trident deterrent, now showing signs of age. None of these countries were anxious to debate all of this on the stage of the UN and so points of order and semantic disputes prevented any serious work being done and the conference broke up in acrimony.

The finger is still on that button: thousands of nuclear weapons remain on hair trigger alert in the US and Russia. These could go off by accident, as a result of human error, or through unauthorized use, perhaps killing millions. We rightly fear the terror of the suicide bomber but the terror of nuclear war could mean suicide for the world.

And if Islamic extremists frighten us, we should be far more frightened by the American Christian extremists who see nuclear war as the divine rapture ushering in a millennium of divine bliss. The stakes are high in this dangerous world where religious ideology can be a blessing or a curse. We had better work hard to make sure that it's the former. [China did not accede to the Nuclear Non-Proliferation Treaty until March 1992. France also did not accede until August 1992.]

In 2006 newspapers printed a letter from 20 bishops asking serious questions about the British government possibly taking the decision shortly to renew the Trident nuclear weapon system. The bishops stated their belief that just war arguments rule out the use of nuclear weapons. Furthermore, they stated that nuclear weapons are a direct denial of the Christian concept of peace and reconciliation.

I did not sign the letter because I do not take quite such an absolutist position. Being one of the generation which grew up under the shadow of the Cold War I believe that it is at least arguable that in those dark days, through the nuclear deterrent, the world was spared a horrific global war, which, even using conventional weapons, could have been catastrophic. Through the grace of God we survived the dangers of the Cold War without the world facing nuclear war. Certainly in the more complicated world of today and tomorrow, it is not clear to me how the upgrading of nuclear weapons adds to our security and I would hope that the decision would not be made solely for the political reason of keeping Britain at the 'top table' of international power-brokering.

The situation five years later does seem a little brighter. A new American administration appears to be taking nuclear disarmament more seriously than its predecessors and a British government has delayed a decision on the renewal of Trident for the time being.

Another issue of public ethics which greatly exercises people at all levels of public life is that of asylum and immigration. The number of asylum seekers in Britain escalated during the 1990s. So government legislation in 1996 tightened up procedures for asylum applications and the entitlement to support. The numbers of applications and the backlog of undecided cases continued to grow. In 1999, the then new Labour government brought in legislation which restricted benefits further, and introduced detention and dispersal. The 2002 legislation tightened even further the culture of deterrence by bringing in stricter rules about benefit entitlement and many asylum seekers were put into destitution: there was an estimated 10,000 in London alone, with women asylum seekers particularly at risk.

The government bills had the effect of many churches and individual Christians and congregations encountering refugees and asylum seekers. Church people with their fellow citizens, engaged in the political arguments, for of course this was and is a deeply political issue. But for religious people this was also a pastoral and a prophetic challenge. Refugees and asylum seekers came to church halls and vicarages because they had few other places where they could go. Their children showed up in Church schools. Clergy were visiting families held in detention centres. Churches, faith communities, concerned people of faith or none were providing food and clothing banks, language and induction classes, were giving housing and legal advice, were providing translations services and generally befriending those confused and lost in a strange land. The stories they heard both angered and inspired and they also discovered that very often asylum seekers brought with them skills, insights and sometimes a deep spirituality.

I sought to put faces to some of the statistics in a 'Thought' delivered in April 1999 when refugees were fleeing the war in Kosovo and Parliament happened to be debating one of the series of asylum bills.

ASYLUM SEEKERS, 20 APRIL 1999

By one of those coincidences the House of Commons yesterday was debating the situation in Kosovo, then later in the week it will be sitting late into the night whilst members wrestle with the proposed provisions of the new Immigration and Asylum Bill. There are those who say that this is an unhelpful coincidence and that the government should delay the debate on its Immigration and Asylum Bill until the Kosovo situation has been clarified. I don't agree. I think that to be considering our immigration and asylum provisions under the shadow of Kosovo can do nothing but good, for if they don't make sense for those fleeing Kosovo, they don't make sense.

Our popular press often gives the impression that Britain is a soft touch for refugees. Let me tell you we are not being overkind. In 1998 almost 35,000 people were removed from the UK – four persons an hour. And whilst they're here they are not being featherbedded. Last week at a refugee centre run by a Baptist church in Croydon I had the opportunity of meeting face to face some of those who have been recently admitted to Britain. Some of the folk I met had been housed in a totally empty flat, with no possessions, furniture, cooker or indeed anything. The good Church people of Croydon work hard to provide basic needs, but it's all very hand to mouth.

Whenever the Bible mentions an ethical social issue it invariably mentions the necessity of treating the stranger within the community with generosity. Why? Because the people of Israel had known what it was to be refugees themselves. At different times they had been in exile in Egypt and in Babylon. The Bible reminds them that God had been with them in their distress and had established them back in their homeland. They should therefore show a particular concern for refugees within their own midst because the moral teaching of the Bible is summed up in the dual command to love God with heart and mind and soul, and love your neighbour as yourself and they had no excuse for avoiding the claims of this particular neighbour.

We can't now claim that we don't know what it's like to be a refugee. The horror of Kosovo unfolding on our TV screens has enabled us as never before to get inside the skin of a refugee. For as we can see these are people like ourselves who've been plucked out of their homes and dumped without documents, money or possessions in a strange land. Through their plight we suddenly see what it's like to be a refugee, and I hope that that gives us the opportunity to look at our immigration and asylum procedures with new eyes.

Loving our neighbour as ourselves may be a little beyond us. But showing ordinary compassion and care in our asylum legislation may be a good first step.

The contribution of religion to public ethics is not solely to argue the moral case for the claim of the distant neighbour on our concern and care, nor is it merely the insistence that seeking justice between human groups and nations is the equivalent of the law of love between individuals. It is also to bring direct experience of pastoral care and concern for those who have been caught up in the grindings of public systems. These systems of control and appeal, emerging from the noble attempt of trying to square the circle between individual human rights and protecting the perceived wider public interest, can (to quote the now Speaker of the House of Lords) be like 'Kafka played by the rules of cricket'.

This chapter started by claiming that public ethics is an extension of personal morals based on the divine command to 'Love your neighbour as yourself', with love and kindness between individuals being reflected as justice between groups. There is a further factor between personal morality and public ethics where public figures are concerned: the question of whether, and how much, a leader's personal life should be taken into account when judging their worth in public office. This is a question which emerges in every decade. The final 'Thought' of this chapter comes from 1993 and introduces the Jewish theological concept of *zimzum*, the ability of a Creator God to give space to his creation and individuals as part of it to develop their own lives without constant pressure.

ZIMZUM, 9 DECEMBER 1993

The question of private morals influencing public life is much in the news. Just how morally pure do we wish the private lives of our prelates, prime ministers, princes or princesses to be? How much is the public entitled to know about those lives, and what methods can validly be used to collect such knowledge?

When I was a student there was a framed notice hanging in the living room of my lodgings. It read, 'In this house the Lord is the guest at every meal, the silent listener at every conversation.' At the time we firmly believed that it was our landlady who was the silent listener at every conversation, but be that as it may. Private morality in traditional religions is partly built upon the belief that God is the silent listener at every conversation, the ever present observer at every act, however private. And if you believe that, then no act is truly private, because God at least is a witness, and to act against your God given conscience before such a witness risks divine judgement. Yet the God who watched and judged was also the God who showed mercy and was prepared to forgive.

Today, private morals, like everything else, have tended to be privatized. Mostly people's consciences are no longer kept crisp and objective by contact with faith communities, and without such contact it is unlikely that we'll see a return to traditional values, for values flow out of faith. A person's conscience today is more likely to be a kind of inner flexible friend, prepared to pay out advice and endorse behaviour which is profitable and which can be got away with.

But that is not the whole of the story, for the privatized morals of public figures today are not as private as they used to be. We have an efficient, ingenious and perhaps overintrusive media whose technology not only collects news and gossip but transmits it widely and instantly. A hint of a story, seemingly private this morning, may well be in everybody's living room, graphically told, complete with analysis and comment, on the one o'clock news. Because of our appetite for such stories, it is the media now who can well be the silent listener at every conversation, the hidden camera at any private act.

But if we're going to play God perhaps we might learn a little from the God which we've mostly displaced. Let's mix a little mercy and forgiveness with our relentless judgement. But perhaps we should go further. There's one religious tradition which sees God's energy and glory before the act of creation as being overwhelming, filling all in all. But on creating the world and humankind God deliberately made space, by withdrawing, standing back, letting humankind be itself. In that way men and women had the chance to grow and develop without being overwhelmed. This gracious way of giving space was given the name zimzum.

I believe that if we want to get the best out of folk in their public lives we would do well to learn a little zimzum, *and like God give some space to people in their private lives. It's more dignified than listening to their every private conversation.*

Zimzum is a helpful notion borrowed from the Jewish tradition. Undoubtably we would all live richer and more fulfilling lives if we could be given the space to do so. The problem is, as Harold Wilson once remarked, 'A week is a long time in politics' and today with instant, global 24-hours-a-day, seven-days-a-week news, an hour is a long time in politics. Those in public life rarely have the luxury of a time of *zimzum*, for events come out of the blue and disrupt their plans. The next chapter will consider this.

5

Religion and Events

Some of the basic questions about God and religion are: 'Why do bad things happen to good people?'; 'Why does God allow war and disasters?'; 'How can a God of love allow a world of pain and suffering?'; 'If God is omnipotent why didn't he devise a world without evil and death?' Behind all of these questions lies a fundamental question about the providence of God and the nature of his relationship to the created world. The question is raised in direct and pertinent ways through particular events. A 'Thought for the Day' is designed to be a theological or spiritual comment on the events of the moment, which of course are mostly unforeseen and unpredictable. It is not too helpful to give general and theoretical answers to baffling events which are all too real. In this chapter we will give some examples of 'Thoughts' attempting to address such events.

Perhaps the most difficult and perplexing question which believers in a good and omnipotent God have to face is raised by the occurrence of natural disasters, particularly when there is extensive loss of life and enormous damage. The tsunami of 2004 was one such event: a gigantic wave, literally coming out of the blue and destroying lives, crops and property all around the Indian ocean. The fact that some of the places were holiday resorts much favoured by Western tourists meant the pictures of the horror were beamed back home as it happened. 'There but for the grace of God goes me,' was the heartfelt response as it had been to the atrocious attack on the Twin Towers in New York. With the latter, however, some human agency could be found to blame, but who is to blame for a natural disaster such as a tsunami, or an earthquake such as those experienced recently in New Zealand and Japan? The insurance companies call such events 'Acts of God', and we're back with the question, 'How can an omnipotent, loving God allow such things? Is there not a design fault in creation?' I began to address such questions in a 'Thought' in October 2005 following a serious earthquake in Pakistan.

EARTHQUAKE, 11 OCTOBER 2005

Such is the severity of the earthquake in Pakistan that there are reports of up to 20,000 fatalities, many related to people in Britain. One consequence of the sad occurrence of so many natural disasters in the past year or two has been the better preparedness of government and relief organizations to swing into action when yet another disaster occurs.

What are we to say? As far as we know, this is the only planet that sustains life and yet we're beginning to understand that we live on a dangerous planet. We build homes and cities on rock plates that shift and move and collide as they float on molten magma. And, as we know, the collisions occasionally result in earthquakes where hundreds of thousands can perish. We're dependent for life on air and warmth and water which form an ecological balance which itself shows signs of catastrophic change. Indeed, we might be near to seeing the end to human life on earth.

Of course we're not the first generation to feel this or ask these questions and people of religious faith over the centuries have tried to come up with answers. For example – that what humans consider evil or suffering is an illusion or unimportant; Or that God's divine plan is good and what we see as evil is not really evil – rather, it's part of a divine design that's actually good. Our limitations prevent us from seeing the big picture. Or that God is a righteous judge: people get what they deserve. Or even that suffering is educational: it makes us better people. Or that evil is one way that God tests humanity, to see if we are worthy of His grace. Or that this world is only a prelude to the afterlife, where no pain will exist.

Well, I don't know whether you find any of that illuminating, comforting or infuriating. The Lisbon earthquake of 1755 – which killed

*100,000 Portuguese people and destroyed 85 per cent of the buildings –
made the philosopher Voltaire question Leibnitz's dictum that 'All is for
the best in the best of all possible worlds' Since the time of Voltaire science
has learned a great deal about the world, but the quest for the meaning
and purpose of life hasn't gone away. Science and religion still have a
great deal to say to one another. We do live on a dangerous planet and
that's not surprising because we're dealing with a dangerous God and
it would be for the good of us all if more people continued to seek the
purposes of God for our world.*

*You may not agree but we can all agree today with the answer the
prime minister of Portugal gave to his king following their earthquake.
'What shall we do?' asked the king in despair. 'Sire, we must bury the
dead and house and feed the living,' was the reply. It's still a good short-
term answer.*

Perhaps we can begin to address the fundamental question, 'How can
a good God allow natural disasters to happen?' by realizing that a
God whose basic nature is one of fidelity and love has not the freedom
to switch these qualities off and act in a capricious manner. In other
words, given God's basic nature, God is constrained by that nature. If,
as Christians believe, the created world is a 'spilling over' of God's love
and fidelity, then its end purpose must be to allow the development of
creatures capable of love and fidelity. The stuff of creation must be such as
to allow the development of life and the only place in the universe where
we have yet discovered life is on our own planet. It is not only that the
earth is positioned just right for life-sustaining moderate heat radiated
to it from the star which it orbits, so the sun can give external energy
for life, but also the internal furnace of the earth's core has made, and
continues to make, its life-giving contribution through volcanoes and the
immense subterranean forces which gradually move tectonic plates. This
still makes the world a mighty dangerous place on which to live, in some
places more than others, but as far as we know such danger is necessary
for life as we know it to evolve. Like an artist or creator, once the medium

has been chosen for the masterpiece, to a certain extent the medium constrains the possible outcome. Once a loving faithful Creator decides to create using material packages of energy and subatomic particles then eventually beings capable of fidelity and love become a possibility, but the material also brings with it change and eruption; a planet without these would be without the most basic forms of life.

Perhaps then it is possible to maintain belief in God's providence in spite of natural disasters, and see the human calling as being to share in the divine project of creating individuals and communities of fidelity and love. But natural disasters are not the only events which put a question mark over such a project; the setbacks usually come through human agencies.

A 'Thought' given in September 2008, quoting Harold McMillan's famous phrase, begins to address events caused by human agencies and relates directly to the title of this chapter.

EVENTS, DEAR BOY, 9 SEPTEMBER 2008

What a world we live in. Recent events have been worthy of a Shakespearean play, though whether a tragedy or a comedy it's difficult to judge. A little over 12 months ago we were in a time of financial stability and gentle growth. In Britain a well respected and cautious Chancellor of the Exchequer had become prime minister after years of planning. In America it was generally believed that Hilary Clinton, again after years of planning, would walk into being the Democratic presidential nomination and probably then the White House. Then a once-in-a-lifetime young, charismatic, sophisticated black American politician appears, upstaging everybody, and no sooner had we caught our breath, when another once-in-a-lifetime, charismatic, young, brash politician appears from Alaska, and she's the first woman to be adopted as a vice-presidential candidate by the Republican party, and all the bets are off for the November elections.

Meanwhile, oil prices shoot sky high and the credit crunch threatens to derail economies on both sides of the Atlantic. In Britain the formerly most financially prudent of governments pours money into rescuing the Northern Rock bank, and then yesterday, in a similar fashion, the most capitalistic of American presidents virtually nation-alizes the morgage giants Freddie Mac and Fannie Mae. Who would have predicted it?

Politics is sometimes a cruel and unpredictable game. Prime Minister Harold McMillan when asked what was most difficult for a national leader to handle, replied, 'Events, dear boy', and with oil crises and credit crunches, and the weather turning violent, national leaders and aspiring leaders have more than enough unpredictable events to deal with at the present time.

It will be of no comfort to them or me to say that it was ever so, but the Bible is so full of unpredictable events occurring, and unexpected characters popping up onto the stage of history, that, not surprisingly, people asked, 'Where is the providence of God in all of this?' What were they to make of one pharaoh in Egypt who made the asylum seeking Joseph his chancellor, or the next who knew nothing about Joseph or his people and pushed them into such cruel slavery that they were provoked to rebel and stride off to seek their own destiny in a land of promise. What were they to make of a later ruler of Babylon who destroyed much of Jerusalem and took its people into exile, an exile where the people of Israel rediscovered their religious roots, or some 70 years later Cyrus the Mede conquering the Babylonians and sending the Jewish people back home again, with their rewritten holy books. Where's the providence of God in all of this?

After world wars and the Holocaust and ethnic slaughter around the globe, it's a question we still ask. Some would be brave enough to say that God doesn't write history, but he communicates with humankind through history, through events, dear boy.

The 'Thought' comes from the time when the unpredicted banking crisis had hit the world, and in America a long-standing Democratic political leader, Hillary Clinton, suddenly had a fierce fight on her hands with

Barack Obama building up a new constituency of support, meanwhile the Republicans were facing a similar surprise through the emergence of Sarah Palin. I referred these contemporary events back to biblical history where the people of Judah and Israel were constantly trying to make sense of an unpredictable history where their life was being constantly disrupted and destroyed. Because of their belief in their covenant relationship with God and their belief in his faithfulness and goodness, the explanation of so many bad things happening to them and their leaders was generally put down to their own backsliding and unfaithfulness and their 'lusting' after false gods. They did not seem to realize that geography was against them leading a quiet life. One of the major routes around the fertile crescent passed close to their land. The land itself was at the boundaries of successive powerful empires: Egypt, Assyria, Babylon, Persia, Greece and Rome. Time and again their cities and buildings were destroyed and some or most of the Jewish people were taken into exile. But events moved on and they, or their descendents, were able to return and rebuild their lives until the final destruction in AD 70 of Jerusalem by the Roman colonialists.

The notion of the providence of God had been shaped by Old Testament narratives of Noah's Ark, the Exodus, the crossing of the Red Sea and the covenant care, punishment and forgiveness of the people of Israel during their history. This led to the belief in God's foresight and power, not only for history as a whole but for events, and in particular, significant events, *kairos* moments, tipping moments in history, where human decisions, under God's providence, could lead to a dramatic redirection for human history. Jesus reflected this understanding in his demand for his hearers to read 'the sign of the times'.

One *kairos* moment for the Jewish people was the destruction by the Romans of their city and temple in AD 70. Another, was their near destruction in the Holocaust in Europe during the Second World War. It would be difficult to see the providence of God this side of those *kairos* moments. In 1947 the world was to see a new state of Israel emerge whose motto might well have been 'Never Again!'

The biblical understanding of God's providence, his foresight and all-directing power, was extended to individual lives. The Book of Job in the Old Testament addresses the question, 'Why should bad things happen to good people?' In the story, God allows Job's faith in his providence to be tempted by disaster. In a short space of time he loses everything: crops, herds, buildings, family. Then pain and illness descend on his own person and he is covered in boils. Still he refuses to curse God or reject his providence. 'The Lord has given and the Lord has taken away, blessed be the name of the Lord' is his response.

Job's 'comforters' bring the conventional explanations for his condition. One tells him that everything will be alright in the long run, that suffering happens to us all so Job should just shrug his shoulders and get on with it. Another says that his suffering is his own fault, so he must confess and repent. Another tells him that he has had a vision which puts everything else into its right perspective. But Job will have none of this: none of these explanations are true or helpful; indeed, they add to his suffering. In my mind, the Book of Job ends without solving the problem of a God of providence allowing the innocent to suffer, but at least it refuses to accept an explanation which this side of the Holocaust would look hollow.

Bad things continue to happen to good people and Church ministers are always tempted to bring false comfort by giving an account of God's providence which denies the extent of the tragedy before them. Such a personal tragedy was the murder of Rachel Nickell in 1992. Here is my 'Thought' of 22 July.

DEATH OF RACHEL NICKELL, 22 JULY 1992

Today the police will reconstruct Rachel Nickell's last walk on Wimbledon Common. My heart goes out to all those caught up in this appalling murder. Rachel's partner has to deal with his own grief. He also has to help the police interview their two-year-old son without overwhelming him with the memory of the cruel attack. And also I think about Rachel's parents. What must they be going through, now knowing that for five days they continued their holiday, unaware that their daughter had been brutally murdered? Some of their feelings came through from Rachel's father at the press conference yesterday.

The clergy are often drawn into situations of personal tragedy. A child, a husband, a wife, a mother meets with an unexpected death. What do you say? I know what I'm expected to say. I'm expected to bring a message of hope and comfort. I know the words. 'Your loved one is now out of pain. Of course you're full of sorrow and regret but don't be sorry for her, for she's gone to a better place. She's with her heavenly father who loves her even more than you.' I know the words, and I believe the words, and perhaps the words bring some comfort. But those words don't reflect what I'm feeling. What I'm feeling is pain, and anger and sympathy, and so I sometimes find myself saying quite different words. In this case, if I were allowed to, I would say words like these, 'This is an appalling tragedy, that Rachel's life should have been cut short in this way when she had so much living to do. It isn't God's will that Rachel should be taken from you like this. We can't explain it. We have no words of comfort. Let's just sit together quietly and weep. But as we weep we can be sure of this. God weeps with us.'

These words I believe are nearer the truth as I feel it. The world is often unfair. Disease sometimes wins, accidents happen, people are brutal to one another, the good indeed sometimes die young. Yet Christians believe that Jesus Christ chose to be in the midst of such confusion and pain. His cross is the centre of gravity of pain and injustice and tragedy. And it is here that God weeps for his son as we weep for our loved ones.

But Rachel's death is more than untimely, of course. Hers is a brutal murder, and I know what I'm supposed to say about that. I'm supposed to speak of forgiveness for the murderer. But I'm not ready for that. Not yet. I'm still too full of anger, and pain and revulsion. Let me share those feelings first. Because forgiveness at this stage would be skin deep. The time for real forgiveness and healing might come, but it lies along the path of justice, and repentance and grief. Now is the time for weeping and anger and now is the time for anybody undergoing such suffering to be held tightly by their friends.

This 'Thought' rejects the offering of cheap comfort in the face of tragic events, but it also questions the notion of cheap forgiveness (particularly on behalf of other people's suffering and pain). I rather wonder, but am not surprised, when Christians, when faced with some appalling crime, wish to express immediate forgiveness to the perpetrator, and then, much later following the trial, express indignation at what they believe to be an inadequate sentence administered by the court. It would suggest that the original expression of forgiveness was not deeply rooted and might have eventually been more authentic if the true feelings of outrage and anger had first been expressed.

Individual tragic events are often symptomatic of a general social malaise. Such I suggested, in a 'Thought' given in April 1999, was the murder of Jill Dando, coming from the underlying trend of increasing social violence.

VIOLENCE, 26 APRIL 1999

Today the murder of Jill Dando is fresh in our minds. Then it's only a week since two nice American teenagers walked into their school and shot 15 of their fellow students. Meanwhile nail bombs go off in Brixton and Brick Lane. There seem to be two common features in all these events. The first is violence, and the second is that the perpetrators of the violence act like God.

In at least two of the incidents extreme violence was used and was carefully planned. Of course America, with its one million guns in teenagers' hands, we write off as a violent aberration. Britain is a more civilized society, or so we think. But we and our children watch the same TV programmes and videos as the Americans, we log onto the same fantasy sites on the internet, our teenagers play the same computer games featuring electronic slaughter. Guns might not be freely available here, thank God, but it would be a brave person who would maintain that our society is not becoming more violent.

I said that our teenagers play the same violent computer games as those in the States; they also listen to the same lyrics of the same rock bands, and one such lyric exactly illustrates the second feature to be found in the violent events of the past week, it goes like this: 'What I don't like, I waste ... What I don't like, I waste.'

When God asked Cain where his brother was, Cain answered, 'Am I my brother's keeper?' In fact, in modern parlance, Cain had wasted Abel. He had acted as his own God and had made up his own moral code, 'What I don't like I waste.' As punishment, God put a mark on Cain, a kind of tattoo. I wonder if he minded. Certainly modern Cains would probably regard such a mark as a status symbol.

But this violence and this making up of our own moral code, relating neither to God nor our neighbour, illustrates something profound which is happening before our very eyes. Traditional societies were bound together by a common belief and a common moral code. In our case Britain was formed partly by the Christian belief and the Christian moral code. In our lifetime we have seen the Christian belief fade, but the pretty people didn't worry too much about that because they told themselves and us, 'What matters is the moral code, and we can have a decent moral code without divine undergirding.'

Well I fear that the moral code might well have been like the smile of the Cheshire cat in Alice in Wonderland which remained for a while whilst the rest of the cat disappeared. In our violent modern world, where each person is their own God, now even the smile of a common moral code is disappearing. Am I my brother's keeper? You must be joking.

The people of Britain are facing a new situation. Past generations were able to refer to a common faith and standards of behaviour. These may have been neglected or ignored, but they were a common moral starting point. Now, with practising Christians being in the minority and also other world faiths being practised in Britain, there is no given common moral reference point as morality becomes detached from religious faith. The challenge is to support those working to find underlying moral standards which can be accepted by people of all religious faiths and none.

In London people have become increasingly disturbed by street violence, particularly amongst young people, with the high-profile murders of Stephen Lawrence and Daminola Taylor being merely the tip of the iceberg. The horror of this is amplified when the victim is a child, particularly perhaps when the perpetrator of the violence is a parent or carer.

VICTORIA CLIMBIE, 29 JANUARY 2003

Last August, rightly, the nation was outraged when two young girls disappeared at Soham and were subsequently found murdered. The facts are, however, that two babies or children are murdered every week by their parents or carers. Mostly their fate doesn't come to public notice. Victoria Climbie claims public attention, not because she was murdered by her carers, but because of the systematic way that she was tortured, brutalized and killed by her great aunt and her partner.

The prime responsibility for her death lies of course with those two adults. They treated her in an evil and callous way and they're now serving life sentences for their crime. Judge Laming, in his report published yesterday points to other responsibilities. A number of individuals in several caring professions, out of fear, inexperience, incompetence didn't fulfil, even the minimum standards of their profession. One gets the impression of a number of isolated individuals on the front line of social care out of their depth as they engaged with a part of the brutal shadow of community life. (We require social workers, teachers, police officers, community nurses to go onto that front line every day.) I know from long experience the strong emotions associated with any allegation of child abuse. A children's social worker is as likely to be pilloried as being an interfering bureaucrat if a child is put into care, as he or she is likely to be criticized if a child, left with its parents, is subsequently injured or killed. We expect often young and inexperienced people to act with the wisdom of Solomon daily.

Now of course no individual should be placed in this position and this is one of the unsurprising conclusions of Lord Laming. He recommends new methods of management so that none of the caring professionals works alone or just within their own discipline. Structures are suggested so that intelligence on a child's condition is shared and assessed.

I'm thoroughly sympathetic to Lord Laming's reforms, but the stark problem which Victoria's murder illuminates for us is that our society in part is sick. A better managed sick society might be a step in the right direction, but it is no substitute for the healing which is at the heart of righteous living. That only comes through changed lives, for you can't renew society with unrenewed people.

Two thousand years ago St Paul wrote, 'Be not conformed to this world, but be ye transformed by the renewing of your mind that ye may prove what is that good and acceptable and perfect will of God.' No structure, however good, can force such inner transformation upon us, but without it all our efforts will fall short.

Another traumatic event involving a young child was the disappearance of Madeleine McCann in 2007 during a family holiday in Portugal. My 'Thought' of 11 September addressed the event. Then, as now, the circumstances of the disappearance were mysterious and the outcome uncertain. Much as we would have wished otherwise, we are not dealing with a God of providence who guarantees happy endings. We are, I believe, dealing with a God whose providence is shown in staying with us in darkness and confused pain.

MADELEINE McCANN MISSING, 11 SEPTEMBER 2007

When I was a young curate I remember being told by a neighbouring vicar, then in his 80s, of the incident which had taken place 50 years earlier which still haunted him. Then, himself a curate, he'd been responsible for the visit of a Sunday school party to the seaside. One child disappeared, and sadly the coach had to return without her. Even though she'd been in the care of her aunt, the young priest felt responsible for her, and even 50 years later, no one knew what had happened to her, and he still grieved for her loss.

You will understand how that story has been much in my mind during these last weeks and months as the story of Madeleine McCann, missing on a family holiday in Portugal, unfurls. We've all been caught up in the horror of this, and our emotions have been pulled this way and that for no one seems to be beyond involvement in this story, from the most seemingly innocent, through suggestions of heavy-handed police, and a whole army of well-wishing supporters and odd eccentrics feeding the media with drops of gossip and innuendo day after day. Nor does the story seem to be abating now that the family has returned to England. And this isn't simply a media led story – for good and positive reasons we feel ourselves to be involved. We want to know what happened.

Of course if this were a fictional story at least we'd be following it in the assurance that by the time we reached the last page all would be revealed. We might be astonished with the revelation of the perpetrator of the crime and the link of events relating to the victim, but all would ultimately be solved. But life is no novel, and, as with my clerical friend and the Sunday school child, there may be no neat ending to the Madeleine McCann story. This isn't good news, but it's the truth. And in this family of faith, where is faith and God in all of this? We might well ask. Occasionally a superman sort of God seems to zap in and solve a tragic situation; more often the God who is present seems to be the helpless God who wept with the disciples as they sat at the foot of the cross grieving the death of his only begotten son.

'Thy Word is all, if we could spell,' as the poet George Herbert put it, trying to fathom the mystery of God's ways. If we could spell. The trouble is we haven't yet learned how to.

The belief in the providence of God does not mean, then, that every human tragedy will have a happy ending. The stuff of life seems to include the possibility of the innocent suffering and the good dying young. God shows his love and fidelity by being alongside innocent suffering rather than preventing it. But that might not be the end of the story. In response to the death of the novelist Douglas Adams in May 2001 I presented a 'Thought' reflecting on the 'inside out' nature of life.

INSIDE OUT WORLDS, 15 MAY 2001

I was very sad to read that Douglas Adams had died at the weekend. His The Hitchhiker's Guide to the Galaxy *books, made all the more popular by their wonderful dramatisation on BBC Radio, were some of the best comic books of the twentieth century. He took really hard scientific concepts and wove them into wonderful stories accessible to everyone. Despite having to overcome writers' block, he made science fiction a new art form. He even came up with the answer to the meaning of life, the universe, and everything. The answer was 42. Through such humour and imagination he created in his books whole fantasy worlds, simultaneously utterly bizarre and completely coherent.*

But there is a point of connection between our everyday world and the world of fantasy which makes fantasy worlds work. Their alternative universes turn the world we live in inside out, and the lives we lead in our world reappear in a different light. It's a bit like dressmaking. You spend hours and hours putting the wrong sides of bits of cloth against each other and sewing them together, and you only ever see the wrong side of what you're making. Then, when you're finished, you turn the whole thing inside out – and suddenly, the right side appears and the beautiful garment is revealed.

Well, perhaps that's not so far from what Jesus meant when he told us that the Kingdom of God is within us. Sometimes, it seems as though we live in an inside-out wrong-sided world. Children kill and are killed, the planet is ravaged and destroyed, wars rage and famine and disease hit across the globe. It has to be said that the great world faiths aren't exempt from this wrong-sidedness either. Many wars have been fought in the name of religion and many atrocities committed. But somewhere at the heart of the Christian faith is the belief that the way we do things now is wrong-sided.

And going with that is the hope that, with the grace of God assisting us, it is possible that the world will be turned inside out and the real glory of the created beauty of the right side will appear. A world put right. A world where none are left out or left behind. A world where good triumphs over evil and where all our wrong sides are joined together and turned inside out. A world glimpsed through the life and works, the death and glory, of Jesus Christ. This is no fantasy world and it won't be realized without a lot of struggle and self-sacrifice, but realized it will be for the Kingdom of God is the meaning of life, the universe, and everything.

The Kingdom of God might well be, therefore, the right side of the project of the providence of a God of love and fidelity, but human beings, working as they do on the wrong side of the project, tend to see life as a terrible mess. This mess is of particular fascination for the media and its customers when public figures are involved. A classic event was President Bill Clinton's appearance before a grand jury in 1998 following his entanglement with Monica Lewinsky, an intern at the White House. I reflected upon the similarities of his situation and that of the great King David back in the sixth century BC.

CLINTON, 22 SEPTEMBER 1998

I've been reflecting upon my own reactions to the Clinton TV interviews concerning his infamous relationship. I say interviews because we've seen two performances in recent weeks: one before a room full of Christian leaders; and the other, a four-hour marathon before a grand jury. Speaking for myself, I thought Clinton the lawyer before the grand jury was more authentic than Clinton the penitent, who won a round of applause from the good Christian leaders but made me squirm with embarrassment.

The Greek philosopher Archilochus wrote centuries ago, 'The fox knows many things, the hedgehog one great thing.' Before the grand jury we saw Clinton the wily legal fox darting and weaving, trying not to be trapped or to say a hostile word about Monica Lewisnky, and to give him his due, he didn't, but in particular we saw Clinton the hedgehog with all his spikes out, knowing the one great thing: that he must not admit to committing perjury – because that would lead to political death.

And the result – a president wounded but still politically alive. An experienced American politician yesterday exactly summed up the situation for me. He said, 'I wouldn't trust the president with my sister, but I'd trust him with governing the country – he's rather good at it.'

There's almost an uncanny similarity between this unfolding story and that of King David in the Bible. He was a fine leader, admired by his people, a skillful diplomat, a ruthless warrior. But he had his personal flaws. He fell hook, line and sinker for Bathsheba even though she was the wife of a neighbour. She became pregnant by him and scandal loomed. Now his ruthlessness was used to his own advantage and David arranged for Bathsheba's husband to be killed in battle. David married Bathsheba and it seemed that realpolitik had triumphed. But no: he was lucky perhaps; he didn't have his relationship picked over in graphic detail by a grand jury and portrayed to every citizen on earth in the name of public morality. But he was challenged by his own holy man, and that was devastating enough. He confessed his sin and was forgiven. But he was never the same man again – tragedy dogged his private and public life.

And yet, and yet … with all his personal flaws, in the judgment of history he was the king to whom the people of Israel looked back to with pride and affection and in later times of natural distress, when they looked for a leader to rescue them, they looked for one who would be – a son of David – a descendant of this great leader. They mightn't have trusted David with their wives, but they would gladly have had him back to rule their country. Clinton is no King David. The question is, is he a good president? The jury of the American people are still out.

During the last few decades Britain has had more than its fair share of events involving the public and private lives of its political leaders, but the events which captured the interest of media and public month after month were those surrounding the breakdown of the marriage of Prince Charles and Princess Diana. When I presented my 'Thought' in December 1994, I spoke of a 'marriage gone wrong'; nobody then had any idea just how dreadful the consequences of all this would be with the tragic death of Princess Diana in the car crash in a Parisian underpass in 1997, and the subsequent outpouring of public grief shaking the monarchy to its foundations.

ROYAL MARRIAGE, 10 DECEMBER 1994

In 1981 I was fortunate enough as an archdeacon in London to have a stall in St Paul's Cathedral. I was therefore present when a tall, shy Prince Charles married his beautiful princess. Archbishop Robert Runcie, conducting the service, called the wedding the stuff that fairy tales are made of, and so it seemed, for the whole nation rejoiced at the couple's happiness. Today the whole nation is caught up in sorrow for a marriage that has gone wrong. The fairy tale marriage of which the archbishop spoke has turned out to be less like Cinderella *where the couple lived happily ever after, and more like* The Wizard of Oz, *where the end of the rainbow turned out to be a little disappointing.*

You'll remember in The Wizard of Oz *how the land was ruled by a magical king, the great and terrible Oz. But when the heroine Dorothy eventually penetrated the heart of his castle, and tore the curtain aside, the Wizard of Oz turned out to be not a magical king but a very ordinary and rather nervous human being.*

That surely is the dilemma for us today with our monarchy. I guess that we still want our Royal Family to be magical kings and queens, princes and princesses, the stuff fairy tales are made out of. But through our powerful media, we can't resist tearing the curtain aside and peering into the heart of their lives, and when we do, it seems that we see a group of men and women having the same problems with marriage as many other people, and having to tackle their problems in the full glare of publicity.

Perhaps we want too much. Just because modern marriage is difficult, perhaps we yearn for someone to have a fairy tale marriage, and so we're disappointed when a prince's marriage hits the rocks. Just because standards of duty in public life are perhaps not what they were, we yearn for someone to give us an example of an unyielding life of duty. Well, we have a queen who has done this for over 40 years; perhaps it's unrealistic to expect the same sacrificial standards from every member of the extended Royal Family.

I'm not one who believes that the monarchy is under threat by recent developments, but it has been wounded and so have we all. And we have all contributed to the wounding by demanding from our media details of the personal lives of our Royal Family that we would not wish to see revealed from our own lives. We have pulled back the curtain of privacy and mystery and shone a spotlight of publicity on people who mostly I believe have been doing their best to give a good example to the nation. I believe that it's time to switch off the light and close the curtain, and give ourselves and them a little peace and privacy.

Christianity is a religion that does not teach that men and women are perfectly good or perfectly horrible. We are all flawed, but through God's grace we can all be drawn to live better lives. We need to give one another encouragement as we seek to do this. Now is the time to give such encouragement not only to our Royal Family, but to those closer to our own homes who are facing personal tragedy and upheaval.

This talk of the flaw in human nature brings to mind the 'Thought' I presented on the day that Robert Maxwell's body was found in the sea off Gibraltar. I had prepared a 'Thought' on a different subject when my producer rang late in the evening with the news that Robert Maxwell had disappeared from his boat and we would need a 'Thought' addressing this. I prepared one and went to bed. I was woken twice during the night, once to be told that a body had been found, and then to be informed that the body had been identified as that of Robert Maxwell. The 'Thought' of 11 November, finally scribbled on the way to the studio tried to give expression to my feelings. Like everyone else I was bewildered, and of course we only knew much later of financial problems including alleged malpractice with pension funds. That particular flaw in this human being was still to be revealed. If the past is a foreign country, the future is a land that is inconceivable. Perhaps that is just as well.

DEATH OF ROBERT MAXWELL, 11 NOVEMBER 1991

Soon after we were married my wife and I went to work in Central Africa. We travelled out be sea on a large cruise liner, the S.S. Vaal, *and had a pleasant enough voyage. On its very next trip a passenger on the* Vaal *fell overboard. Nobody missed him for several hours but then the ship turned around, and despite the vagaries of current and wind, the man was found still alive in the warm tropical waters. Yesterday Robert Maxwell was less fortunate; it has been reported that he was dead before his body was found.*

It's a truism to say that one day we'll all have to die, but as a parish priest I often used to reflect that the manner of a person's death not infrequently reflected the manner of their life. For example, quiet, brave people often endured painful final days quietly and bravely, whilst fighters would fight their disease and would continue to fight often to the point of death.

Robert Maxwell died dramatically and mysteriously, and in doing so captured the headlines of the world. It was a larger than life death; he was a larger than life figure. He was a millionaire socialist, a publisher and newspaper proprietor who was not too coy about using the pages of his own newspapers at times as a mouthpiece for his clearly expressed views. A passionate football follower, everything he did, he did to the limit. He didn't just write for newspapers – he owned them. He didn't just support football – he bought the club. He loved life to the full, drained every drop of excitement from it, and along the way contributed not a little to the richness of life of many of his fellow citizens. Like everyone else, I'm not at all sure what to believe about the circumstances of Robert Maxwell's death, but it certainly reflects his life.

Whatever his beliefs, a man who had seen many of his closest family die in a concentration camp would have known these words from Psalm 103: 'The days of man are but as grass, he flourishes like a flower of the field; when the wind goes over it is gone; and its place will know it no more. But the merciful goodness of the Lord endures for ever toward those that fear him; and his righteousness upon his children's children.' I hope that words such as these are bringing some comfort to the family of Robert Maxwell today, for a big man has been cut down.

Instantaneous judgement of current events is always a hazardous business. Politicians can call upon historical precedents but history never quite repeats itself and when it comes to the behaviour of individual human beings, each is quite unique, and the character of each is often hidden within layers of personality and pretence. The great religions of the world are great because they have survived and proved to be of value in different times and cultures. They also have a healthy scepticism about the behaviour of individual people, knowing them to be capable of acting as angels or devils. The New Testament promises that there is nothing hidden that will not be revealed. Our judgements on 'events, dear boy' must always therefore be a little tentative. Humility is a good quality for the social or religious commentator.

6

Religion and Science

I have inhabited both the worlds of science and religious faith during much of my ordained ministry, particularly in its early days when, after ordination and a few years in parochial ministry, I served a dozen years of so as chaplain and lecturer in electronics, first at the University of Zambia and then at the University of Kent at Canterbury. Throughout my ministry, the worlds of theology and science have overlapped and, over time, my attitude to both has changed. If, when I was studying and teaching science, I managed to snatch opportunities for reading theology with almost a secret thrill, since becoming archdeacon and then bishop the position rather reversed. Now, the thrill is picking up the latest science magazine or paperback, and for me God is as likely to impact on me through either and, in particular in the overlap of these worlds.

Albert Einstein famously wrote, 'Science without religion is lame, religion without science is blind'. He realized that in a world it is essential that people of faith, and of no faith, work together with scientists for a future of hope rather than of despair. I referred to Einstein in a 'Thought' which I presented in July 2005 marking the planned collision between a space probe and a comet deep in space.

EINSTEIN, 4 JULY 2005

A hundred years ago this week, a patent clerk in Zurich, Albert Einstein, was having a waking dream, a vision of what the world would look like to someone riding on a beam of light, and travelling near the speed of light. Out of his dream he articulated the theory of relativity, a new description of the world of the infinitely big and the infinitely small, which turned mathematics and physics upside down. Dreaming at his desk, he saw the world, not as others see it, not just the externals, but rather he saw the world in depth, multidimensional, more wonderful, more terrible than had ever been conceived.

Had he been here a hundred years later I'm sure that, yesterday, he would have been captivated and would have shared the delight of scientists around the world as the deep impact spacecraft beamed back pictures of the collision between its space probe and comet Tempel 1. The collision matters because it's got under the skin of the comet and thrown up material which can be analysed and examined, and that matters because comets aren't just giant dirty snowballs. They contain materials that have remained largely unchanged since the formation of the solar system 4.6 billion years ago. Understand those building blocks and we might get a clue as to how life emerged in our corner of the universe.

This is long distance science recording an impact 83 million miles away. Yet such is its significance that it evoked wonder in the hearts of its designers. Wonder is something that religion knows about. Elizabeth Barrett Browning once wrote, 'Earth is crammed with heaven and every living bush is aflame with God. But only for those who take off their shoes, the rest sit around and pluck blackberries.' Of course most of the time we don't see the awe of the world aflame with God. We don't have the eyes to see God continually creating and recreating the universe and indeed ourselves. We don't have the imagination of an Einstein or a Browning to see past the externals into the very heart.

In the mid-nineteenth century the great scientist James Clark Maxwell sent a postcard to his colleague James Joule who'd achieved a breakthrough in physics. The postcard read, 'There are very few people who after great mental and material toil have been able to put their mind in exact accordance with things as they really are.' That's the calling and the excitement of science, to put one's mind in exact accordance with things as they really are, and yesterday's triumph is a great example. The calling and excitement of religion is even more demanding – to put one's mind, and heart, and soul, in exact accordance with things as they ultimately are in a universe aflame with God.

In this 'Thought' I refer to several features which I believe are common to science and religion. Firstly a common experience of truth and awe. If science handles truth through that which can be measured, and religion works with truth that comes to us through story, poetry and imagination, prayer and worship, both pursuits know, from time to time, the feeling of awe. Professor Eric Laithwaite (who invented the electric liner motor) once said, 'When measurement after measurement clicks into place around a successful hypothesis it is a deeply awesome experience.' Then there is the common attempt in the perceptive words of Maxwell to Joule for the scientist 'to put one's mind into exact accordance with things as they really are' which might be developed into the objective of the life of religious faith 'to live in accordance with things as they ultimately are'.

I tried to tease out the overlaps and the distinctiveness of science and religion in a 'Thought' 'Bumblebees Can't Fly', broadcast in October 1990

BUMBLEBEES CAN'T FLY, 9 OCTOBER 1990

I enjoyed hearing the interview last week with the scientist who'd discovered, by using the latest mathematical techniques, that bumblebees can't fly. He hinted that he had another idea which might explain the flight, but the interviewer, despite his skill, wasn't able to extract that theory from him. Fortunately, nobody has told the bumblebees about this and so they continue to fly with their minds at rest.

One shouldn't blame the scientist for this hard-headed approach to the flight of the bumblebee. It's the scientist's job to assemble knowledge, fact by fact, small step by small step, building new theories upon firm ground; and it's this kind of approach which, on the following day, sent a spacecraft spinning its way to examine unknown regions of the sun. But accumulating facts is not the whole of science. There's plenty of room for imagination and creative vision.

For example, Copernicus turned the medieval world upside down by asserting that the sun, rather than the earth, was at the centre of the universe. He would have appreciated the space flight, but in fact, he came up with his creative vision without discovering any new facts. He simply saw the same old universe as everyone else, but he saw it in a different way.

In our own time, Einstein, sitting in his office chair in Zurich, merely asked himself, 'What would the world be like if we were riding on a beam of sunlight?' A ridiculous question: the kind of a question children ask until they grow up, but out of that question and others like it came the theory of relativity and space travel, and atomic power, and the magic of the computer chip.

I'm not one of those, then, who would want to claim a total distinction between a religious and a scientific approach to the world, because respect for truth lies at the heart of both, and both leave room for leads of imagination. And who would have thought that a scientific book on modern physics would top the best-seller list for months on end, but Stephen Hawking's A Brief History of Time *is up there, not only because it's good science, but because it's full of awe and wonder.*

It's not necessary then to pick a flower or a bee to pieces in order to understand the world. There are other approaches to truth which are equally valid, which attempt to see the world, not in pieces, but in tune; for example, the beauty of a violinist at one with her instrument in a Beethoven concerto; the awe with which a parent holds a new baby; the rapt attention of worshippers gathered around the altar and focusing upon a truth beyond themselves.

We can only know that kind of truth when we stop treating life as merely an object, and start treating it as a gift, and I believe, a gift from God. As the Psalmist says 'The heavens declare the glory of the Lord and the firmament shows God's handiwork.' So take comfort fellow bumblebees, spread those wings and although they tell you it's impossible, just fly!

There is an important distinction between science and religion, however. Science proceeds by framing a hypothesis about some aspect of reality and then designing apparatus so that, through careful measurement, the hypothesis can be tested; in religion the hypothesis takes the form of a personal faith in God and the believer is the apparatus and his or her life is the experiment. In both, however, the quest for truth is taken with utter seriousness and neither science nor religion need be afraid of following their particular paths and disciplines towards truth, wherever they may lead. The theologian Simone Weil wrote, 'Christ prefers you to follow truth to following him, for Christ is truth and if you follow truth you cannot avoid coming to him.'

Traditional science handles truth by taking very seriously what can be measured. Experiments are carefully devised and the results accurately reported even when the results might indicate that a hypothesis has proved to be inaccurate; the location and accurate description of a blind alley can be just as significant as a confirmation of the truth of a hypothesis. Both can move science forward. The important thing is that the experiment is repeatable, and through scrupulously accurate reporting, other scientists may test the claims for themselves. Through this, the pursuit of scientific truth is a corporate activity. This goes some way to explain the shock in the scientific community when in 2006 the claims of a well known Korean scientist, Woo-Suk Hwank, proved to be false. I presented a 'Thought' on 4 January 2006 referring to this and developing the ideas that rigour and truth and the testing of what is good and true belong also to the realm of religion, otherwise humanity might repeat the mistakes of past disasters.

SCIENTIFIC CHEATING, 4 JANUARY 2006

Shortly before Christmas the Korean scientist Woo-Suk Hwang announced that he wanted to withdraw his latest published scientific paper. In Korea he has had the status of a pop star as, over the years, he's claimed remarkable results in stem cell research holding out the hope of regenerative therapies for people paralysed or suffering from such diseases as Alzheimer's, Parkinson's or diabetes.

But science has a system of professional peer scrutiny which ultimately uncovers false or exaggerated research claims, and the results that Woo-Suk Hwang claimed were too good to be true. It seems that they were fakes, coming not from genuine research but from manipulation of images. In his own words, 'The research paper contains fabrication and needs to be retracted.'

This has left the stem cell research world in some confusion. Woo-Suk Hwang's work had seemingly been so much more productive than that of others, that fellow scientists around the globe had stopped what they were doing and attempted to follow in his footsteps. Now it's impossible to know whether the research had any authenticity or not. Months, perhaps years, of other work which might have been more productive have been wasted, and the hopes of those seeking to relieve suffering have had a severe setback. But there's something more fundamental to which we should attend at the start of a New Year. Trust in the truthful reporting of rigorous research lies at the heart of true science. Without this the scientific project collapses. There's already anxiety that for commercial reasons much scientific research today takes place behind closed doors and is never reported at all. Now this high-profile case of fabricated research adds to the worries of those anxious that scientific standards are slipping.

Scientific research just can't go forward without rigour and truth. The negative result of an accurately reported experiment is just as useful as one which has proved positive, because through it fellow researchers learn that this is an unproductive line and attention can be directed elsewhere. There's then no need for others to go down the same blind alleys.

Rigour and truth matter beyond the realm of science. In politics and religion, for example, our impulses can thrive on false sentiment, emotional need and cultural manipulation. In its search for meaning, the mind is apt to go down some wrong paths and to mistake its own reflection for the face of God or the new Messiah. Often this doesn't do too much harm but occasionally we see a Jonestown, a Waco, or fanatical suicide bombers. The experimental results of the great religions teach us that we need neither follow such extremists down blind alleys, nor destroy our way of life in reaction to them. Let that be our truth in 2006.

The idea of the oneness of truth has always been at the heart of Christian thinking. As a Christian I can look for, and expect to find, aspects of truth in both science and religion, but they are often different faces of truth. I do not have to believe in the literal truth of the Genesis story of creation for example, because the Book of Genesis is not a science, history or geography book; it is handling a different aspect of truth.

I accept that the scientific theories of big bang creation and the evolution of life give us great insight into the creation of humanity and are, in their own terms, just as exciting and inspiring as the Genesis story. But that does not mean that the religious Book of Genesis does not also contain profound truth. Genesis is the fruit of the reflection of the people of Israel on the triumphs and disasters of their history and the attempts to answer fundamental questions. If the big bang theory postulates the 'How?' of creation, Genesis attempts to answer the 'Why?' There is nothing particularly new in this insight. Back in the fifth century, St Augustine of Hippo wrote, 'The Bible does not teach us how the heavens go, it teaches us how to go to heaven.'

It is instructive to compare and contrast the scientific and biblical stories of creation for I believe that each has much to learn from the other and each can add value to the other. The big bang creation hypotheis sees the big bang – at the start of time and space some thirteen and a half billion years ago – creating in a big bang something out of nothing. The 'something' was very strange indeed: a big bang exploding from a pinprick of searing heat and incredible density until the laws of physics kick in after 10^{-35} seconds and exponential inflation occurs and the building blocks of the simplest atomic nucleus coalesce. As the universe expands and cools, we move from a time scale of micro seconds to a time scale of billions of years. The first galaxies appear after a billion years or so, with our sun in its galaxy of the Milky Way appearing nearly five billion years ago. Then comes the earth with its moon, the first oceans, single-celled life some three and a half billion years ago. Then we are into the hundreds of millions of years time scale, with fish, land creatures, dinosaurs, birds, mammals and humanity branching out in the tree of life. We see then an ordered creation out of nothing but following the laws of physics over both incredibly small and then incredibly large periods of time.

The story as told by Genesis also sees creation out of nothing; but it is no accident, rather a purposeful creation because God wills it. Before there is anything, we are told, the Spirit of God brooded over the dark void, rather like the laws of physics brooding over the primeval big bang chaos. It again is an ordered creation in the writer's mind over a period of six days, with the procession remarkably similar to the evolution of the galaxies and then life forms as in the scientific theory. But, at the end of each day, the Creator reflects and says, 'That's good.' And, on the sixth day, humanity is created 'in our own image'. We can share something of the mind of the Creator and his joy in his creation as he observes, 'That's very good.'

I returned to the question of the nature of the universe in a 'Thought' of April 2007, referring to a scientific report from Italy claiming that, far from being cosmically smooth, the universe is fractal-like, with clusters of matter or energy at every level, large or small.

FRACTALS ALL THE WAY UP, 24 April 2007

In the introduction to his book A Brief History of Time, *Stephen Hawking tells the story of the scientist giving a public lecture on astronomy. At the end a member of his audience told him that what he had said was rubbish. That in fact the world was a flat plate supported on the back of a giant turtle. The scientist gave a superior smile before asking, 'And what is the turtle standing on?' 'Well,' came the retort, 'you think you're very clever, but its turtles all the way down.'*

I don't know about turtles all the way down, but according to a recent scientific report from Italy the universe is fractals all the way up. Fractals are familiar enough in nature. For example, consider the structure of a tree: zoom in and zoom out and the same pattern appears again and again at every level – the whole tree, a branch, a twig, a leaf.

And so, it is claimed, is the enormity of the universe. Far from being smooth, some regions contain clusters of matter. There is no argument that the universe is far from smooth at relatively small scales like clusters of galaxies, but what is now being claimed through new and more powerful surveys is that the cosmos looks fractal-like all the way up, or all the way out, and this conflicts with the standard model of a smooth universe at its ultimate limits.

Well, we can leave the cosmologists to their arguments, but they have an uncanny similarity to the arguments which theologians have had over the centuries about the ultimate nature of God – the smoothness of one ineffable, awesome reality, or the cluster of persons in community. After many battles the Christian understanding became both: three in one, and one in three – the Trinity. Three persons in an ultimate community.

That might sound very abstruse and theoretical, but if that is the ultimate reality of God, it is not surprising that that same pattern shows up fractal-like all the way down, to every human community, to every human person – our nature is the oneness of personal responsibility yet one that is formed and lived out in community. What the balance should be is a question of political argument both here and particularly in France, at the present time.

People neither lock themselves out or are locked out from the good community. All have a place and all have a contribution to make. The shape of our community helps or hinders this, for the truth is that individuals make the community and the community makes individuals. The virtuous fractal occurs when the individual is good for the community and the community is good for the individual. How we do that is called politics.

If science strives to tell the 'How?' of creation, and religion the 'Why?', I believe that we need both and can have both. There is nothing in the big bang and the Darwinian theories that gets in the way of my religious belief in a transcendent God who, out of pure goodness and will, created space and time out of nothing and as part of the package created the laws of Physics, which then make creation make itself.

Of course, not everyone would agree with me. I suppose that the contemporary scientist best known because of his skills in communicating atheism with evangelistic zeal is Richard Dawkins. The dispute between him and some religious believers has all the elements of a revisit to the dispute between Charles Darwin and some of the Christian leaders of his day over the theory of evolution, which, in turn, had echoes of the still earlier dispute between Galileo and the Vatican over his theory of a sun-centred universe rather than the theologically approved earthed-centred universe of the day. Those of us trained in both science and theology tend to groan at the pointlessness of these unnecessary disputes, which, overall, have so much undermined the authority of the Church.

Certainly Darwin himself found the disputes between the religion and science of his day distressing. In a letter to a friend he wrote, 'I hardly see how religion and science can be kept distinct, but there is no reason why disciples of either school should attack each other with bitterness.' I would go further and claim that science has developed in the West because it has been built on the foundations of Christian religious principles of the value of the created world and the importance of rigorous thought.

Science and religion in conflict may still be the position of the 'person in the street' that is articulated clearly and with conviction and passion by Richard Dawkins, but I believe that over the past century the situation has become less certain, even though the 'person in the street' might not catch up with this thinking for some decades yet. Since the beginning of the twentieth century traditional science has been challenged by a 'new physics' that describes a world which is very strange indeed. Sir Arthur Eddington put it this way: 'It has been the task of science to discover that things are very different from what they seem.'

I believe that it is significant that Richard Dawkins is a biologist and that biology – and its children – has been one of the most successful of the 'old sciences'. But it's the discipline of physics that tries to delve into more fundamental levels, and it is the 'new physics' – delving, through quantum mechanics, into the incredibly small and, through relativity, into the incredibly large – that has been discovering that existence is more mysterious than we imagine or can imagine. Niels Bohr, one of its exponents, has said that, 'Those who are not shocked when they first come across quantum theory cannot possibly have understood it.' The quantum world really is different, and the only way to come to grips with it is to suspend some of the beliefs and the disbeliefs of traditional science. It is as though the edifice of science and technology has been carefully and logically constructed brick by brick to produce the most impressive structures, only to discover that the foundation upon which all this is built is decidedly shaky.

The writer, Annie Dillard, has put it this way: 'For some reason it has not yet trickled down to the man in the street that some physicists now are a bunch of wild-eyed, raving mystics. For they have perfected their instruments and methods just enough to whisk away the crucial veil, and what stands revealed is the Cheshire cat's grin.'

I touched on the relationship between the 'new physics' and religion in a 'Thought' following an Easter meditation by Pope Benedict in April 2006.

PHYSICS AND RELIGION, 18 APRIL 2006

Pope Benedict was rather fierce in one of his Easter meditations. Seeing the world in the grip of Satan and praying for mankind to open its eyes to what he called the filth around us, he expressed fears about genetic modification and said that it was insane arrogance to play with the grammar of creation.

Now there is no doubt that there are scientists today who pursue their calling with the fervour of a Christian fundamentalist, but it would be sad if there were to be a return to the suspicious hostility between Christianity and science which damaged both in the centuries following the discoveries of Galileo. In fact, scientists and religious believers underestimate how many of the essential beliefs about the natural world on which modern science is based have stemmed from basic Christian beliefs – that the world is good, rational, orderly, open to the human mind, and to be understood and developed for the common good. Such beliefs have shaped our culture through the centuries and have provided the necessary seedbed for science later to develop and prosper.

Neither is arrogance the normal attitude of the research scientists. One, probing the mysterious world of quantum mechanics, talks of 'physicists as an occupational hazard spending a large part of their lives in a state of confusion'. He claims that to excel in physics is to embrace doubt while walking the winding road to clarity, but nothing comes easily for nature doesn't give up her secrets lightly.

Another probing the equally confusing world of the vastness of space, ponders that, 'As we look out into the universe and identify the many accidents of physics and astronomy that have worked together for our benefit, it almost seems as if the universe must, in some sense, have known that we were coming.'

Nor is the hostility to religious faith which marked some scientists of past generations common today. Scientists have learned to be less dogmatic. One speaks of matter as 'weird stuff, weird enough, so as not to limit God's freedom to make of it what he pleases.' The spat between the Church and Galileo was foolish and unnecessary. A much earlier Christian Scholar, St Augustine, had encouraged the study of nature and the search for nature's laws. As well as the book of the Bible written in ink he spoke of the book of nature 'Look above and below, note, read. God whom you want to discover did not make the letters with ink; he put in front of your eyes the things that he made.'

Today, with satellites and space shots, atom-smashers and quantum probes, new knowledge is coming at bewildering speed. It's not the time for scientists and people of religious faith to lose touch. We need the insights of both.

One of the scientific hypotheses yet to be proved is that of dark matter. It seems that what we can today observe and measure in the universe is far too small to explain why the universe sticks together and behaves as it does. There must, it is suggested, be a vast amount of dark matter also existing that, by definition, we cannot see. And the latest cosmological theory goes further. It suggests, in addition, a 'dark force' to explain why the universe is now expanding more quickly than it should. It is postulated that there's a dark force combating gravity and pushing things apart. This has led Wendy Freedman, writing in *The New Physics*, to say, 'The measurements point to a universe filled with a kind of matter which we've never seen, propelled by a force which we don't understand.' And then they say that religion is all faith!

Or perhaps the Bible will try to help us out, for Christians many centuries ago were told by St Paul: 'Now we see through a glass darkly. Then we shall see face to face.' So perhaps we need not get too disturbed at living through a universe filled with a reality that we have never seen, propelled by a Spirit that we do not understand.

I learned a little of 'seeing through a glass darkly' some years ago, in a trivial and yet profound encounter with my first personal computer which included a chess programme. It was pretty crude and the computer was extremely slow by today's standards. I typed in my move, then the screen went blank for a few seconds whilst the computer thought and then it displayed its move. The programme had five levels of difficulty and, as I started at the bottom level, after a while I began to win quite frequently. The computer stepped up to the next level of difficulty. This was indicated by the fact that the screen went blank for a longer period between moves. The computer was taking more time to analyse and plan and, when it did make its move, it invariably won the game. And so on through the levels with the screen staying blank at the top level for several minutes. Now a casual observer would say, 'Why are you looking at a blank screen; nothing is going on, something has gone wrong.' The reverse was the truth. A great deal was going on behind that blank screen, and nothing was wrong. On the contrary, the darkness was an indication that I was developing more skill in my chess playing.

So it is, I would argue, when we are wrestling with the most funda-mental questions in science, humanities or theology. Courageously staying with a darkness we do not understand and find difficult to penetrate is sometimes the precursor to fresh insight – the WOW experience of new insight does not always come cheaply

St John of the Cross writes of the 'Dark Night of the Soul', not as something going wrong in our relationship with God, but as an inevitable part of Christian maturity. We should neither be disturbed by the dark mysteriousness of God nor overexcited by any glimpses we might have of glory. I always smile at St Theresa's response to the novice who burst in upon her, spilling out an account of a glorious vision that she had just received. 'Never mind, my dear,' the saint retorted. 'Go on with your prayers it will soon go away.'

I find a helpful image of the dark impenetrable side of God is the black hole. The black hole, as you know, is a type of star that is so massive that its gravitational force prevents anything – even light – from leaving its neighbourhood. Light and matter can go in but nothing can come out. The qualities of the black hole cannot be probed directly but they can be discerned by their influence on everything else. Here, relativity and quantum mechanics both have their part to play, as do theology and poetry.

For this notion of a black hole being so real and so massive that it can only be discerned through its effects on everything else has echoes for me of the language of Christian mystics who for centuries have been saying precisely the same thing concerning the nature of God's awesome reality. It cannot be observed directly – for it is too massively real for human understanding – but can be discerned by its influence on everything else.

If the black hole is infinitely dense, what is revealed when the new physicist probes deeply the infinitely small, for example the smallest unit of matter? Is it a particle or is it a wave? Well, both and neither. Let Richard Feyman explain: 'If I say they behave like particles I give the wrong impression; also if I say they behave like waves. They behave in their own inimitable way, which technically could be called a quantum mechanical way. They behave in a way that is like nothing that you have ever seen before.'

This talk, of a world of 'potentialities rather than certainties', has raised religious questions for another physicist, Freeman Dyson. He writes: 'Speaking as a physicist, scientific materialism and religious transcendentalism are neither incompatible nor mutually exclusive. We have learned that matter is weird stuff. It is weird enough, so that it doesn't limit God's freedom to make of it what he pleases. We stand … midway between the unpredictability of matter and the unpredictability of God.'

Most people now have heard of that uncertainty principle: the principle that we just can't be certain about every aspect of matter in its most basic forms. For example, if we know an electron's velocity we cannot know its position and, if we know its position, we cannot know its velocity. Uncertainty is built into nature. Albert Einstein found it very difficult to accept the uncertainty principle. He said, 'God doesn't play dice with the universe.' But, within the uncertainty principle – and using the disciplines of mathematics and probability – quantum physics has been remarkably successful in explaining, testing and predicting basic truths. So much so that a response to Einstein's axiom has been, 'We are dealing with a God who plays with loaded dice, capable of driving creation towards higher and higher degrees of spontaneous order.'

This has led some scientists to ask basic questions once more about the form and the origin of the universe and its realities – with some surprising results. For example, Sir James Jeans has written, 'The universe can be best pictured as consisting of pure thought. If the universe is a universe of thought, then its creation must have been an act of thought.' The opening of the Gospel of John, I believe, puts it more succinctly: 'In the beginning was the Word'.

The 'new physics' tells us that we have on our hands a world of possibility and potentiality – a world that can be probed provided we set aside our everyday perceptions. It is a mysterious, awesome world but not totally hostile to the human enquirer. Indeed, it seems, as Freeman Dyson has written, 'The universe knew we were coming.'

The physicist Professor Paul Davies takes this a stage further in what he calls 'The Goldilocks Enigma'. He addresses the fundamental question, 'Why is the universe on our side? Why is it just right for life? Like Goldilocks – not too hot, not too cold, but just right.' This is quite a miracle the professor explains: were the laws of physics and the values of fundamental qualities to be only minutely different from what they are, existence as we know it would be impossible and certainly there would be no life. I raised issues such as these in a 'Thought' on 29 January 2008.

RECREATING LIFE, 29 JANUARY 2008

Where does life come from, what is its status, and can we recreate it ourselves? These are questions buzzing around the scientific community at the present time, and lest we think they are theoretical questions, there's a whipped government bill leaving the Lords this week on its way to the Commons opening the door to radical new developments in embryology, and a team of scientists in America believe that they are well on their way towards the synthesis of an entire bacterium which they would plan to put into an empty cell and produce synthetic life.

Well, if that thought is a little overwhelming for this early in the morning, let's start with life as we know it and attend to what some are calling the Goldilocks questions. Why is the universe just right for life and human life at that? Why are the laws of physics and the value of fundamental constants exactly what are needed to a fraction of a percentage in every case for chemicals and then life to emerge? It's as though the universe knew we were coming. Perhaps it's just a fluke. Perhaps there are billions of other parallel universes with different properties of which we can know nothing, because by definition we inhabit the universe whose laws and properties are life friendly; if they weren't we wouldn't be here asking the questions.

To someone like myself who inhabits a world of religious faith but takes an interest in the things of science, it is intriguing how many mental gymnastics some people will go through coming up with more and more improbable suggestions rather than consider the rather obvious hypothesis that perhaps the universe is life friendly because it's designed that way. A universe with thoughtful self-reflecting life forms like ourselves is infinitely richer than a world of sterile darkness.

Of course, Christians believe in just such a Creator God but that doesn't mean that we have to accept the biblical poetry of creation as scientific truth: it's perfectly possible to believe that God created the universe to create itself, and I do.

But are there any limits to this self-creation? The human genome is now mapped out in DNA code – chemical word after word as it were spelling out the how and why and when of life. In the beginning was the Word, the good book says, and the divine Word spoke and there was life. Can it really be the case that soon scientists will create synthetic life through arranging the basic words of the DNA code? Speaking for myself, I am both awestruck and frightened at the prospect. For example, computer-designed synthetic bacterium that gobbles up carbon dioxide might be a solution to global warming, but such bacterium getting out of hand and gobbling up all carbon dioxide would mean the end of life. Goldilocks won't always protect us.

I had raised the question of the dangerous unintended consequences of scientific developments almost 20 years earlier in a 'Thought' given in July 1991 called 'White Rabbits'.

WHITE RABBITS, 9 JULY 1991

When we lived in Central Africa my children had a beautiful white rabbit living in a hutch on the veranda. Late one evening we heard a terrible commotion and went outside to investigate. The rabbit was going wild. I shone my torch and was shocked to find that the rabbit was no longer white. It had turned black! Then I saw that it was covered with a multitude of large black ants, the vanguard of a countless army of ants marching towards the house. Unless I acted quickly the rabbit would merely be the first casualty. Fortunately, the previous week we had stocked up with a crate of cans of insect spray. I first sprayed the rabbit but then it took the contents of a great number of cans before the ant army could be persuaded to change direction and turn away from the house. We sighed with relief for without the rabbit's warning the first we would have known about the arrival of the ants would have been when they invaded the baby's bedroom.

Now this was before the world knew of such things as the threat to the ozone layer, lead-free petrol and the like. I was just grateful to the chemical company who'd provided us with a weapon to protect our house and children. Now, we're better informed and, rightly, green issues are high on our global agenda. Yesterday our prime minister launched one initiative and the Labour party launched another. But we'd be fooling ourselves if we were to believe that such initiatives are likely to be problem free. In these green times I often wonder just how I would have dealt with the situation in Africa without the use of chemical spray. I suspect that we'd have had to give way to the ants and the rabbit, at least, would have been doomed.

The abandonment of chemical farming, the conquest of pollution, the reduction of energy levels, are all going to be costly to implement. I'm not at all sure that, in order to preserve long-term life on our planet, we'll be prepared to pay the necessary price of a reduction in our standard of living. After all, we certainly haven't been prepared to lower our standard of living to help those in the developing world, by paying a proper prince for their copper, coffee, tea or sugar. So perhaps our enthusiastic support for green issues is a little premature; let's wait until we've seen the bill and voted with our plastic cards to pay it.

Christian theology is not totally optimistic about the capacity of human beings to make sacrifices. Christian teaching tells us that we have a fatal flaw in our make-up which means that we don't always act sensibly, even when it's in our interest to do so, and indeed the selfishness which eats away at the soul can be even more fierce than the black ants which would have eaten away our white rabbit. But that is not the whole of the story, for Christians also believe that the grace of God is deep at work within us, pulling its weight in the battle between generosity and self. If our new concern for green issues finds its true source in these gracious levels of the human spirit, then there is hope that we will be able to act out on the conviction that nature doesn't exist simply for our benefit and pay the necessary price which might save our grandchildren's world.

The next chapter will develop further the questions which technology, science and religion raise concerning the issues of life and death, but this chapter ends with a 'Thought' from December 1993, called 'Hubble – Correcting the Flaws'. The magnificent Hubble telescope to everyone's consternation turned out after it was put into orbit deep in space to have a flaw which made its images useless. It says much for humanity's capacity to screw things up that a telescope which took decades to plan and construct and costing millions of dollars could have such a flaw. We realized that modern science and technology is not foolproof; things can go wrong. But also, it says much for the human spirit and skill and ingenuity that a further space mission could be devised, planned and executed which corrected the flaw, enabling sharp, colourful, wonder-filled images from deep space to be beamed back to earth for over 17 years. After the date of my 'Thought' humanity had to hold its breath for six weeks before the first pictures came through, proving that the correction had worked; a late but very welcome New Year present to the world.

The 'Thought' takes the story of the Hubble vision and the correction of Hubble's flaw as a parable for the correction of humanity's moral flaw and humanity's vision lived out in the lives of such people as Martin Luther King and Mother Theresa. The last sentence of this 'Thought' might also describe the scientific and religious visions at their best: 'Such glimpses build new worlds with heaven in them.'

HUBBLE – CORRECTING THE FLAWS, 7 DECEMBER 1993

Today the astronauts on the Endeavour *space shuttle are into the fifth day of their flight to repair the Hubble space telescope. Actually, they have to do better than repair it. For the telescope has never worked properly from day one. It seems that its mirror was flawed, ground too thin. True, it is only 10,000th of an inch out, but that's enough for its images to be blurred and smeared. So the main purpose of this week's flight is to place corrective lenses over the mirror. Hubble will be wearing spectacles from now on so that it can see clearly and sharply.*

St Paul talks about humanity having a similar flaw in our moral seeing. Now, he wrote, we see through a glass darkly. Now our knowledge is partial. It's this flaw in our make-up which makes Churchmen and women a little reluctant to be too judgemental of their fellows, or claim too much certainty. An Eastern sage put it another way: 'He who speaks. doesn't know. He who knows, doesn't speak.' Speak we must, of course, if we're to be of use to one another by sharing insights and faith, but if a 10,000th of an inch in the Hubble telescope makes all the difference between clarity and blur, so the smidgen of distortion in our moral make-up is not to be ignored.

It's taking a $629 million mission to correct and counteract the Hubble flaw, not to mention the risk to the lives of seven astronauts. But the bravery, skill and cost will be worth it, if the spectacles work because humankind will then have the opportunity of seeing the cosmic heavens in a totally fresh and wonderful way. Through Hubble we'll be able to peer into the depths of quasars and plot galaxies bursting into life.

Christians believe that the correction of humanity's moral flaw was even more costly, yet produced even more wonder-filled results. It might be simplistic to see the life and death of Jesus Christ as a divine rescue mission designed to cure humanity's spiritual myopia. Yet the effect was precisely that. As the Christmas story is told and retold, heaven touches earth, whilst the cross of Christ provides humankind with new moral optics – so that men and women can see visions and dream dreams.

St Francis had a vision of a grace filled world where even the birds and the beasts were brothers and sisters to humankind, and his wandering friars took that vision into the towns of medieval Europe. Martin Luther King had a vision, had a dream of a world where black and white people walked hand in hand, and he bussed that dream around the southern states of America. He died but his dream lived on. Mother Theresa's vision includes even the destitute and the dying amongst whom she lives on the streets of Calcutta. These are all men and women with a clear vision, seeing through the optics of the divine.

We're told it will take more than six weeks before we know whether the correction to Hubble has proved to be effective. The Christian faith may have lasted 2,000 years but it has to be tried and tested anew in every generation in every life. Flaws there still are aplenty, but there have been glimpses of wonder-filled clarity which have turned the world upside down. Such glimpses build new worlds with heaven in them.

The worlds of quantum physics and cosmology are awesome, and wrestling to understand them can be mind-blowing, but scientific developments impinge more intimately upon individual people in matters of their life and death. The next chapter will examine some of these.

7

Religion and Medical Ethics

If astronomy and cosmology probing the infinitely large, and the 'new physics' quantum mechanics probing the infinitely small, have raised new ethical questions in our time, similar advances in the medical sciences have raised new questions, literally, of life and death. The 'new biology' of genetic engineering is making discoveries and asking questions new to humanity. This chapter will address some of these questions, but by revisiting some of the 'Thoughts' of the last couple of decades we will be reminded of just how rapid the developments have been and just how difficult it is for religions whose faith is centuries old to address new questions which were not only not on the agenda of faithful people of previous ages, but would have been quite beyond their comprehension.

This perhaps is one of the reasons why people become so passionately committed to one view or another, particularly in the field of reproductive or regenerative medical research, and argue their various cases through pressure groups of one sort or another. Even those of us less at home in such polarized groups, however, can nevertheless recognize that there are real and disturbing ethical issues.

The most basic ethical issue is that of unintended consequences of any technological developments. Some consequences can be anticipated. They may be intended or desired; they may be not desired but probable; they may not be desired but improbable. These anticipated consequences can be thought through in advance before the experimentation proceeds. What is more difficult is the unanticipated consequences, which again, when they occur, may be desirable or undesirable. During the twentieth century we have seen sufficient examples of undesirable consequences of conventional technologies, whether they have been a result of careless maintenance in a chemical or nuclear plant, or the unanticipated effect of asbestos dust on the human lung.

If the unintended consequences of conventional technologies can be devastating, how much more might they be in the world of medicine where the materials have a life of their own and can respond to any modification in sometimes unpredictable and unsafe ways. We need, therefore, to be hard-headed and clear sighted about the potential risks of medical research whilst being equal aware that the possible gains are enormous as we have seen in the eradication in the West in the last 50 years of killer diseases, through the development of penicillin and antibiotics. Today, by experimenting on a human embryo or an animal, medical science might eventually come upon a cure which will save the lives of many But where there is no guarantee of a successful outcome, the life and dignity of the patient actually before the doctor or medical researcher is of supreme importance and must weigh heavily in the balance of whether or not to proceed into unknown territory despite the potential gains which might result for future human wellbeing.

There are not infrequently then good ethical arguments for proceeding with a piece of medical research and good ethical arguments for not doing so. This is why, ultimately, it is the judgement of the whole community through Parliament, faiths, the media and pressure groups, and not just the judgement of the medics, which decides what is, and is not, legitimate research at the present time. It is not only some actual believers in the divine who get anxious about humanity 'playing God' with the human condition, but it is hard to maintain this argument in its purest form. Other developments in science and technology have rather overtaken it. Not to interfere with the human condition would rule out most modern medicine and surgery not to mention other environmental and social changes. Most Christians have long ago accepted that our imagination, insight and skill are part of the God-given realities of the human condition and are to be used to better the lot of individuals and society.

Environmental and social changes already alter, in effect, the genetic composition of future generations. Advances in medicine, agricultural changes, the taxation system, aid relief, social trends all have their effect in determining the nature of the next generation of families. Much of the genetic impact of these changes might well be unconscious. With genetic engineering the genetic impact is intended. Enzimes are used to add or subtract from a length of DNA. Many would accept that, with careful monitoring and control, such developments are legitimate when used to eliminate a genetic effect causing a particular disease, provided there are no objectionable side-effects. There are a huge number of genetic diseases with physical or mental effects. Some are quickly lethal, others kill more slowly if at all. Some are painful, others not. The number of diseases having a single genetic cause seems to be disappointingly few but Huntington's disease or spina bifida seem to be amongst them, and it is difficult to see a moral objection to attempting to remove the offending gene from future generations. But accepting this limited and particular use of genetic engineering does not lead necessarily to accepting other uses such as attempting to produce what is thought to be desirable characteristics in perfectly healthy people.

I dipped my toe into some of these issues in 1995 with a 'Thought' triggered by the development of a 'smart bandage' but which also referred to the decyphering of the DNA of a living organism, which, of course, has changed the whole landscape of medical research and ethics ever since.

SMART BANDAGES, 1 JUNE 1995

Medical science has had a busy week. Scientists at Glasgow have just announced the development of the smart bandage. It's made of a bio-compatible plastic which, when bound around a wound, accelerates the healing process. It's a step along the way to further developments in cellular engineering which will produce smart dressings and clips which having helped the body to heal itself will dissolve away without leaving a trace.

Well, nobody could argue with that; it's an obviously useful development. But some people might have more anxiety about the implications of another medical development announced at the weekend. For the first time the complete DNA code for a living organism has been deciphered. If I understand this correctly, it means that it is now possible to identify all the key elements necessary for the life of a particular bacterium.

Now this might be seen to be of limited practical value except to the bacteria concerned, but in fact it gives tremendous encouragement to those hoping that medical science before too long will be able to target defective genes in the human person, or manipulate them in such a way that even a disease like cancer might be at last understood and conquered. But the thought of genetic engineering sends shivers down the spine of some people. The cry goes up, ' We shouldn't interfere with nature.' The same cry opposed the development of anaesthetics, blood transfusions, and inoculations. Indeed, some people objected to giving pain-relieving drugs to mothers in childbirth because they argued that the pain of child-birth was one consequence of Adam and Eve's rebellion in the garden of Eden and so to seek to relieve it was to obstruct the will of God. But I believe that God makes creation make itself, and humanity as a conscious and intelligent part of creation, despite the dangers, is capable of cooperating with its Creator in bringing healing to a good, though wounded world.

Indeed, medical science has interfered so successfully with nature in our own lifetime that we've seen the conquest of major killer diseases such as measles and whooping cough. The new frontier to be tackled now is the 6,000 human diseases having genetic causes.

But there are dangers. The best technology can be misused. For example, in some parts of the world genetic screening, which provides a powerful method of spotting some genetic defects in young foetuses, can also be used to eliminate the birth of a perfectly healthy baby whose parents perceive it to be of the wrong sex. Society needs to be aware of the dangers, and governments have the duty to encourage, enable and control the development of these new genetic technologies if they are to prove to be a blessing rather than a curse. We can safely leave the use of smart bandages to the medics. But we'd all better take a smart interest in the new genetic developments – there's a great deal at stake.

Such was the speed of development that within five years the complete description of the human genome was published. President Clinton immediately announced that the genome sequence could not be patented and should be made freely available to all researchers. The result was that the scientific community downloaded one half-trillion bytes of information from the genome server in the first 24 hours of free and unrestricted access to the genome server. Important parallel research was taking place developing the sequencing in the DNA of other organisms such as mice, fruit flies, yeast and plants, but it was work with the human genome which naturally caught the public imagination, for it offered tangible benefits. My 'Thought' of 27 June 2000 examines some of the implications, again sharing the excitement of the possibilities for the good of humankind through this development but also flagging up the dangers of unintended consequences and the need to be vigilant.

THE HUMAN GENOME, 27 JUNE 2000

It is being claimed that 26 June in the year 2000 will in later years be seen to be a hinge of history. Why? Because on that day the human genome was published. Until yesterday, historians were telling us that for humans there have been three ages of development – disaster, disease, decay. Most people, for most of history, died rapidly though disaster – cold, hunger, violence. Then more recently (and still today around the world) disease has been the agent of death. Now in the West the age of decay is upon us, when most people die in old age. But from 26 June 2000, if the more prophetic scientists are to believed, a fourth age becomes a possibility: the age when humans have the power to conquer most disease and prolong life indefinitely. Perhaps.

The description of the DNA letters of the book of life of the human genome, all 3 billion of them, is now known, but what do those letters precisely mean? Which bundle of DNA molecules form which of the 40,000 or so genes, and which of these in turn cause which characteristic of the human character to malfunction? That is the enormous challenge to be tackled. And it's only when this is understood that the cure for genetic disease can be sought, a further major challenge. It's probably best not to get overexcited then, for the fruits of this wonderful research may take some time to ripen and perhaps that's just as well, for we need time to think them through. We've learned from experience that science can produce a mixed basket of fruit. Some fruit never ripens. You remember the wonderful Zeta project that was going to harness the power of the H-bomb and produce endless electricity at minimal cost and no risk? The science was known but the technology proved impossible. The fruit withered on the vine.

Then there's fruit that goes badly wrong – we're still suffering from the scars of BSE. Then there's fruit which comes from science misused, and there's plenty of opportunity to misuse the human genome project. For example, new forms of eugenics where unborn children thought to be less than perfect for any reason could be eliminated, or genetic discrimination could become commonplace in the fields of employment or insurance, amongst others.

Religion teaches us to have a respect for the integrity of creation. In recent times we've come to see that God creates, by making creation make itself. From 26 June 2000 comes the possibility of this part of creation, humanity, remaking itself. But in whose image, and for what purpose? We may have answered the 'How?' but have we answered the 'Why?'

Some of the fruits of the publication of the human genome became quickly apparent. It turned out that there is an estimated 20–25,000 genes in the human genome, far less then had previously been thought. Then it was surprising just how many genes humans have in common with other species and how relatively few genes are specific to the human animal. Furthermore, out of the three billion DNA letters which describe each human, only some 10,000 distinguish it from another human being. Genetically, it seems that we are all almost identical twins. One conclusion is obvious: as the great religions have always claimed, we are brothers and sisters sharing a fragile world with other creatures, our cousins, for which we have a duty of care. It also follows that the behaviour which distinguishes us from our neighbours to a large extent flows from ourselves and from our environment rather than from our genes. It seems that the doctrine of human 'free will' was more accurate than we had realized.

Nowhere have the developments in medical science been more rapid than in the field of human fertilization and embryology, and no subject has engendered more debate and dispute, for it touches on deep human beliefs and feelings. The basic driving force has been the wish of a woman to have a baby when there are medical or other reasons for her not to be able to do so. Some have seen childbearing as a basic human right, whilst others have been disturbed at what they see as unnatural medical technology interfering with the God-given way of birth.

In vitro fertilisation, IVF, has been the medical vehicle seeking to overcome problems of infertility. The process involves hormonally controlling the ovulatory process, removing ova or eggs from the woman's ovaries and letting sperm fertilize them in a fluid medium. The fertilized egg or zygote is then grown into an embryo and then transferred back to the woman's uterus and hopefully to a successful pregnancy. The first successful birth of a 'test tube baby' occurred in 1978.

Because of the sensitivities of these developments in Britain all human embryos created outside the body are subject to regulation. The Human Fertilization and Embryology Act in 1990 laid down strict guidelines, including the length of time that eggs can be stored in a frozen state for possible later use. Although eggs have been successfully unfrozen and utilized after ten years the Act stipulated a maximum storage period of five years. This watershed was first reached in 1996 and my 'Thought' of 23 July, 'Decisions, Decisions', addresses some of the ethical questions raised by this.

DECISIONS, DECISIONS, 23 JULY 1996

'Quick decisions are unsafe decisions.' So said Sophocles two and a half thousand years ago, and he didn't have to face some of the most difficult and complex ethical decisions which come our way today

through medical research, none perhaps more difficult than the status of frozen embryos. The starting point was simple enough: through the development of in vitro fertilization new hope of having children was brought to many childless couples. Eggs were fertilized in the test tube ready to be transferred as embryos into the womb of a recipient mother. But because such IVF usually produces more embryos than can be put back into the womb, tens of thousands have been put into cold storage.

The present law states that such frozen embryos, no bigger than a pinhead, can't be kept longer than five years unless their parents consent to further storage. And next week over 3,000 of these (originating from parents who either can't be traced or who have refused to reply) reach the five-year watershed. What are the clinics to do? Many Christians believe that human beings are created at the moment of conception, so for them the answer is simple – to destroy an embryo is to destroy a human being. But what of those of us who don't take this absolutist position and yet are unwilling to treat the embryos merely as pieces of redundant flesh, to be destroyed at will. The problem is that because these are new technologies it is impossible to find detailed guidance either in the Bible or in the classical theologians.

However, I am helped by the ethical principle of proportionality. Applied here, it would suggest that, whilst treating a potential human with respect, the protection given to a human embryo should increase as it grows. With an embryo of four cells having minimum protection and a foetus capable of independent life having the full protection of any other human being. The logic of this position is that those embryos next week could ethically be destroyed, but that still leaves me feeling very uneasy, and I suspect that that is right and proper, for when we cease to feel uneasy about these modern ethical decisions we have ceased to be human.

Five years remained the maximum permissible storage time for frozen embryos in Britain until 2009 when it was doubled. In 2010 a woman in

America gave birth to a healthy baby using an embryo which had been frozen for 20 years.

The concept of increasing protection as the foetus grows is a useful ethical argument in resolving the polarized positions of those who claim, for example, in arguments regarding the morality of abortion, that the embryo has the full protection of a human being from the moment of conception and those who believe that the foetus has no protection until the moment of birth when the new baby has full protection. With billions of embryos being naturally aborted early in pregnancy and with babies being born long before the pregnancy has run its course and with advanced medical care proceeding to a healthy childhood, both polarized positions run contrary to common sense. The 'increasing protection' concept, however, seems ethically reasonable and is similar to the position held by earlier Christian moral theologians such as St Thomas Aquinas who did not regard the abortion of a foetus to be murder unless it had reached the point of being 'animated'. The exact age at which this occurred was debatable. This question of the status of the foetus was further raised with the real prospect of foetuses being produced which could then be used as a source of parts for transplanting to a profoundly sick sibling. This, of course, could come as great good news to some parents and children but it also raises the ethical question as to whether we should treat something that has a capacity to become a human being as a source of spare parts. Is the foetus merely an object or does it have dignity in its own right?

The Human Fertilisation and Embryology Act might have controlled and guided developments in the UK, but other possibilities were becoming available in other parts of the world. A 'Thought' which I presented in October 1999 discussed the implications of couples purchasing 'eggs on the internet'. Behind my concern is the thought that if soon it becomes possible for only a genetically fit embryo to be implanted in the womb, the next step could be designer babies, and no doubt fashions in what makes a desirable baby would change just as fashions in everything else changes. If a child grows up knowing that its parents had designed it, might it not resent what it has become? My 'Thought' returns to the basic principle that the prime question to ask is always 'What is in the interest of the child?'

EGGS ON INTERNET, 26 OCTOBER 1999

The internet is a growing marketplace, but who would have thought that couples, desperate to have children, will soon be able to purchase maternal eggs on Ron's Angels Web Site. And these aren't any old eggs. These are eggs supplied by American models and they cost somewhere between $15,000 and $150,000, perhaps depending upon the colour of the eyes or the hair. This new initiative for designer babies reminded me of the story told, I think, by George Bernard Shaw, when the technology wasn't so advanced. A famous actress approached him and suggested that they should marry, 'For,' she said, 'just think how wonderful our children would be with your brains and my looks.' 'But madam,' the great man replied, 'how dreadful if they had your brains and my looks.'

I suspect that someone paying even $150,000 might not get the precise designer child they'd hoped for. If parents are always a disappointment to their children, and they are, children are always more demanding than expected; they never conform to the design in the fond parents' minds. I remember a young mother saying to me, 'I so much wanted a baby, but all she does is cry.' Well yes, babies do cry, usually in the middle of the night. They haven't designed one yet, even for $150,000 that doesn't, and to quote a certain Fran Lebowitz, 'All God's children are not beautiful. Most of God's children are barely presentable.'

Well, that might be so, but, young or old we're all children of God, and the Good News of the Christian faith is that God that doesn't love us because we're good, or even presentable: God makes us good because he loves us. On this basis the great religions might have a few precepts which could be of use to a new generation of parents. First, never forget that moment when you held your baby for the first time – you knew then that this was a wonderful, mysterious gift; it still is, even when it cries in the middle of the night, or throws its food on the floor. Second, don't expect babies and children to set you off well, like a living fashion accessory – if you do, as sure as fate, they'll let you down. Third, it's hard, but try to ask, what is in my child's interest, rather than what's in mine.

Of course the great religions have been around a long time in all sorts of cultures and they know what's in a child's interest. I'm afraid it isn't fashionable but it's this: simply to grow up in a stable home, where the parents show love for one another and the children in good times and bad until the kids are grown up. To create such a home is far more valuable than spending $150,000 on the right eggs.

The 'eggs on the internet' saga did not go away, however, with a British graduate in 2010 offering her eggs for sale for £4,500 to help pay off her student debt. A spokesperson for the Human Fertilisation and Embryology Authority, which regulates egg donation, said that prospective patients seeking donations should only use licensed clinics. Another specialist warned prospective egg donors that selling eggs is like selling an organ: it involves taking a lot of medication which, in rare cases can have serious side effects.

IVF by this time was becoming quite an industry with purpose-built clinics and hospital wings staffed by clinicians confident about their growing expertise, providing this service for parents desperate to have children. I was becoming worried that some basic questions about the intended and unintended risks of IVF and assisted pregnancies were being overlooked, not least the real tragedies of some children whose parents had been aided by IVF being born with serious deformities. In some cases there was very little feedback between the clinician caring for a badly deformed newly born baby and the consultant who had supervised the IVF. Indeed there was a culture of denial because the successes were also dramatic and few people wanted to consider the shadow. A related further step was taken with the cloning of 'Dolly the sheep' in 1996 and the claim by a certain Dr Zavas in 2004 that he had implanted a cloned human embryo in a woman. I took advantage of this news story in January 2004 to raise the anxieties I had about the lack of transparency concerning IVF outcomes.

ASSISTED PREGNANCIES, 19 JANUARY 2004

Dr Zavos, the fertility doctor, has caused a stir by his claim that he has implanted a cloned human embryo into a 35-year-old woman. To attempt such a feat in the UK would be illegal, perhaps for reasons suggested in a comment by Dr Reik, a cloning expert in Cambridge, who says, 'My view is this man is exploiting the emotional pressures of parents desperate to have children.' But even if this and other moral objections were to be ignored, there are good medical reasons why the treatment should be outlawed, for according to Dr Reik in every single experiment attempting cloning in animals 99 per cent die in the womb and the other 1 per cent have problems.

But the fact is that at the forefront of any medical treatment, there is a danger that the difficulties are underestimated by all concerned and I don't think that I'm alone in getting anxious that this is happening across the board of the assisted pregnancy world – IVF and associated treatments. Anything concerning the creation of human life is of especial concern to people of faith who believe such life to be a gift of God and I acknowledge that assisted pregnancy units can boast of some wonderful results – healthy babies born of grateful parents, but those of us who go in and out of hospitals know of the grief and heartache which are also to be found: frequent miscarriages, birth defects and associated problems as the baby grows and develops.

Lord Robert Winston, a pioneer of IVF treatment has recently said, 'If you are using treatments that might damage somebody – such as an unborn child – then you have a duty to tell people.' It could be that the shadow side of the assisted pregnancy industry has been underestimated in recent years. There are possible reasons for this. Not only do doctor and patient so much wish the technique to work that they play down the possible dangers, but it's hard to get hold of firm statistical data, so that the risks can be weighed, and it can happen that there is little feedback from the paediatric surgeon who seeks to treat the serious birth defects in the newborn child or infant and the medical team responsible for encouraging the pregnancy months before. They might well be proceeding to treat the next set of patients, blissfully ignorant of the difficulties their previous patients are facing in another part of the health trust.

But there is a theological defect called wilful ignorance, which the medical profession like others has a duty to avoid. 'There is nothing hidden which will not be revealed', the gospel of Luke tells us. The Medical Research Council embarked on a massive study on IVF safety last year. Let's hope that all will be revealed.

In the event it was January 2011 before the Human Fertilisation and Embryology Authority (HFEA) published its review of scientific studies into health risks of children born through IVF, which indeed indicated a higher risk of giving birth to children with low birth weight, neurological conditions such as cerebral palsy, cancer of the retina and heart defects. The overall risks might still be small but they are significant and HFEA believes that clinics have a duty inform patients of the consequences and risks of treatment.

To return briefly to the question of human cloning mentioned in the Thought; Dr Zavos's claim proved to be too ambitious, for it soon emerged that the attempt had not succeeded and the woman did not become pregnant. Human cloning attempts do have their supporters with the claim that in this way, through therapeutic cloning, genetically identical cells could be provided for regenerative medicine and tissues and organs for transplantation which would not trigger an immune response. It is claimed that serious diseases such as cancer and heart disease might benefit from this technology. Others go further and would wish to see a cloned child replacing the generation of the clone of a previously living person. The technology is fraught with risk, however, not least that of producing a prematurely aged child. Reproductive cloning is banned in most countries although some allow research into therapeutic cloning.

It seems that constant ethical vigilance is necessary in matters of birth, but in past decades equivalent attention has been given to death, with just as much dispute and disagreement, for the other issue of medical ethics which has been constantly on the moral agenda is that of assisted suicide. The argument from human rights is similar to that regarding abortion. There it is claimed that a mother's life and body is her own so surely she is free to decide whether or not to abort a foetus which is a part of her body. It is nobody else's business, or if it is, her voice must be the deciding one. Equally, when it comes to the question of suicide the argument runs: if a person's life is his or her own, he or she has the right to end it when it is no longer a life they wish to live. And if they, through incapacity, are not able to perform the fatal act without help, at their request they should be able to be assisted by a sympathetic person. In Britain suicide ceased to be a felony in 1961, though to aid or abet suicide remains an offence.

The traditional Christian position is somewhat different in both cases. It is that each person's life is a gift from God and that a person is not its absolute owner. A mother is not the absolute owner of the foetus: the foetus deserves protection in its own right, although this might be a developing protection as the foetus grows in the womb. When it comes to suicide, traditional belief is that our life is entrusted to us in order that we may each find fulfilment in the service of God and neighbour. Deliberately to destroy one's life is therefore a sin against God through the rejection of his love, and an offence against humankind. This, of course, is without taking into account the impact of the long-lasting grief and guilt survivors might be forced to endure. I suggested in my 'Thought' of January 1995 that suicide, tragically, often comes out of losing a sense of proportion and allowing sometimes some quite trivial matter to so dominate one's feelings, so that life is felt not to be worth living.

SUICIDE, 25 JANUARY 1995

An art gallery in Glasgow is showing a rather strange exhibition at present – a collection of suicide notes. Visitors disagree about whether or not such an exhibition can be classified as art, but many have been profoundly moved by their visit. One note comes from the pen of a 12-year-old boy who had shot himself. It reads, 'Dear Dad, Don't feel sorry or sad. I lied and lied. I got an F grade in English … Much love, Pete.' How truly awful. Every parent putting pressure on a child to do well in exams needs to read that and ponder. But that tragic note, I believe, has a wider significance. It's a warning about what happens when we lose a sense of proportion and let one disappointment or setback grow until it blots out every other aspect of life, or even life itself.

An argument at home, a lost opportunity at work, the end of an affair, the loss of a pet, a worrying ache or pain, a burglary, a car smash; the list of setbacks which can come our way is endless, and it is easy to let any one of them get out of proportion and take us into a spiral of depression or anger. And it's not only individuals who can get into such a spiral: groups, Churches, societies and nations can fall into the same trap. A political party is quite capable of tearing itself apart by focusing on a single issue which is then emphasized out of all proportion – Britain's place in Europe, for example, or a clause in a party's constitution. And getting things out of proportion isn't merely a British disease: in Groznia we've just seen a city bombed into oblivion to keep a satellite within a crumbling Russian empire.

The writer of the biblical Book of Ecclesiastes was a wise, if cynical, observer of human affairs. He advocated the living of a balanced life, a time to plant and a time to uproot, a time to weep and a time to laugh, a time of mourning and a time of dancing, a time for silence and a time for speech. St Benedict some 700 years later built a whole community on the basis of living a balanced life, Work, worship, study, fellowship all had their place, and none dominated. But there was one thing which was certainly out of all proportion in that faith community and in the faith communities to be found in our own cities, towns and villages today: the sense of the love of God overflowing in ridiculous abundance, and enfolding and bearing up the lives of foolish, unbalanced, sometimes fretful women and men. Once we get a sense of that disproportionate love it's not necessary for us to write suicide notes.

If in practice today, both within society and the Church, suicide is treated with compassion, occurring when the balance of mind, heart or soul is disturbed, with organizations such as the Samaritans providing a listening ear to help prevent the calamity of suicide, there is less agreement about assisted suicide. It is understandable that a person suffering from a debilitating disease, feeling that they are no longer the person they were, and becoming totally dependent on others for their life and welfare, might literally feel that life is no longer worth living. Of course such feelings might vary from day to day and may also be dependent upon the mood swings consequent on drugs given to alleviate pain. Such people deserve and receive great sympathy, as do those caring for them, but the law in Britain, as yet, has not given permission for another person to help them in a suicide attempt.

Several attempts have been made during the past decade, both at national and European levels, to liberalize the law so that a person, usually the partner, who assists in the suicide of someone terminally ill would not risk prosecution. Diane Pretty, suffering from motor neurone disease, was such a case in 2002. The European Court of Human rights had refused her request that her husband should be immune from prosecution. In my 'Thought' I welcomed this, pointing out that if the law wavers in such hard cases then the lives of many vulnerable people might be affected. It is a supreme example of ethics taking into account the effect of actions on the 'distant' neighbour. There are real concerns that if the law changes 'the right to die' would risk becoming 'the duty to die'.

DIANE PRETTY, 30 APRIL 2002

I was once visiting a ward in a nursing home caring for some very frail elderly people. They were predominantly female, but as I stood and found my bearings an old man beckoned me across. I regarded this as gesture of male solidarity and went to hear what he had to say. 'You're standing in front of the television,' he complained. The world occupied by sick elderly people can be a worrisome place, and it's not easy, when you've always led an active life, for your care now to be totally in the hands of others. And more often than not there are things to worry about with home and family, if you still have a home and family. I've lost count of the number of times an elderly person has said to me, 'I don't want to be a nuisance. It would be much better if I didn't live much longer.' People say these things, and they partly mean them. They don't want to be a nuisance to their children and grandchildren. They don't want to see their house sold and their savings used on costly care for themselves. But when frail people say that they don't want to be a nuisance they are also very often, I believe, looking for reassurance. They are wanting to know that they're still valued and loved. They're wanting to hear that their wisdom and experience still matters. They're wanting to be assured that their life is still worthwhile.

That's why I for one am rather pleased at the decision of the European Court of Human Rights to refuse Diane Pretty's request for her husband to be immune from prosecution if he assists her in committing suicide. Of course Diane and Brian Pretty have our compassion and sympathy. Theirs is a very hard case. But hard cases make poor law, and if the law wavers over assisted suicide or indeed euthanasia then very many vulnerable elderly people of the type that I've mentioned will feel themselves to be under great moral pressure no longer to be a nuisance to those around.

Law and religion see eye to eye on this. Human life is a gift from God which must be respected. We don't have the authority to take away life, even our own. The judges in Strasbourg are quite right, therefore: human rights legislation protects the right to life, not the right to death. Of course the Prettys like all of us have the freedom ultimately to follow their conscience, having weighed up the rights and wrongs of their situation, but none of us can escape the consequences of our actions even when we feel that we are following our conscience. There are no post-dated moral cheques in this sacred journey through life and death.

Diane Pretty died a month later in the care of a hospice and, of course, the founding and support of such hospices has been one of the most dramatic developments in medical and nursing care during the past few decades. Pain control is now better understood and the effect of drugs on mood shifts and the acceptance of 'living wills', where a terminally ill person instructs that he or she is not to be resuscitated, have brought more peace of mind to a person approaching death. It is a fine example of the adage from the nineteenth century poet Arthur Clough, 'Thou shalt not kill but need not strive officiously to keep alive.'

A move to make it legal to help a terminally ill person to die was defeated in a free vote in the House of Lords in July 2009 but the argument made in the debate by the former Labour Lord Chancellor, Lord Falconer, that the present legal 'no man's land' required clarity was later taken on board by the Director of Public Prosecution who published draft guidance in February 2010. His advice lists a range of factors that would be taken into account when deciding whether a prosecution is appropriate or not. These include whether the 'victim' had reached a voluntary, clear, settled and informed decision. There is particular emphasis on the motivation of the 'suspect' who must have acted wholly compassionately. The DPP stopped short of offering guarantees but he sent strong signals that a person helping a terminally ill loved one to die would not face prosecution.

Developments in medical science have placed before us new possibilities for the human spirit and new questions about life and death. These basically religious questions about how to live and how to die are emerging from the sciences whether or not the scientists themselves have any religious faith. I pointed to this new reality in a 'Thought' given in June 2008 after I had shared a TV platform one Sunday morning with Richard Dawkins. Terry Pratchett, suffering from a rare form of Alzheimer's disease, would later in 2010 in giving the Richard Dimbleby lecture argue powerfully for a tribunal to be set up to look at an individual's case for assisted death. He ended the lecture by saying 'If I knew that I could die at any time I wanted, then suddenly every day would be as precious as a million pounds. If I knew that I could die, I would live. My life, my death, my choice.' But in my June 2008 'Thought' I focused on an earlier incident which he had shared in a newspaper article which raises basic questions about life and death.

TERRY PRATCHETT, 10 JUNE 2008

A few weeks ago I found myself on a TV Sunday morning programme where Richard Dawkins was a fellow panel member. He probably won't thank me for saying so, but I found myself more often agreeing with his responses than with some of the wilder Christian members of the audience, not least over the casting out of supposed demons from children. I was reminded of the new King William of Orange's answer to the person asking for the traditional sovereign's healing on Maundy Thursday, 'May God give you better health and more sense.'

But the strange fact is, that it is often writers like Dawkins and Philip Pullman who would regard themselves as atheist who touch on some of the most profound and basic religious questions. In Dawkins' case, the necessity or otherwise of a divine Creator of a wondrous and awesome universe; in Pullman's case, the tension between human free will and social control or the interface of parallel universes.

An even more moving example was covered in one of the Sunday papers. That astonishing writer Terry Prachett has sadly been diagnosed as having Alzheimer's disease. The report records that he says that he is an atheist but after his diagnosis something happened. He was rushing down the stairs one day when, to use his words, 'it was very strange, and I say this reluctantly, because I am trying to deal with this situation in as hard-headed way as I can. I suddenly knew that everything was okay and I thought, well that's alright then.' Did it make him rethink his lack of faith? Well, to quote him again: 'It's just possible that once you have got past all the gods that we have created with big beards, just beyond that on the other side of Physics, there just may be an ordered structure from which everything flows.' But he winds up, 'That's both a kind of philosophy and totally useless. It doesn't take you anywhere. But it fills a hole.'

I think that it does rather more than that. The medieval mystic Julian of Norwich during one of the outbreaks of the Black Death in England, and when she herself was grievously ill, experienced a vision of a hand gently holding a hazelnut which she likened to God upholding and enfolding the world and, like Pratchett, she just knew, that, in her words, 'all shall be well, and all shall be well, and all manner of things shall be well'.

Escapism – perhaps. A meaningless psychological delusion – it's possible, but to the person experiencing it, nothing is more real or significant or disturbing. I've learned much about life and religion from Prachett's books and hope for many more, but for his sake and mine I hope that the most significant truth of all is that despite pain and terror, ignorance and stupidity, disease and death, despite all of these, everything is ultimately okay.

In countries like Britain it used to be thought in the 1960s that religion was an echo from a previous age which would soon disappear, as public life no longer needed or used such a hypothesis as the existence of God. That has not been the experience in the last years of the twentieth century and the first decade of the twenty-first. Religion is now very much part of the fabric of modern life. How does this affect our systems of education? How do we best educate our children in a new world which is always changing yet where some old ideas and concepts appear to be timeless? The next chapter will focus on religion and education.

8

Religion and Education

I suppose that if there is one subject which the Church of England is supremely well qualified to talk about, it is the subject of education. The Church has been involved in education since its earliest days. Schools founded by bishops and run by cathedral clergy were set up in England between the fifth and eighth centuries. Originally founded to train priests they were soon admitting lay students. Meanwhile, Benedictine monasteries were also becoming centres of learning, and by the eleventh century 35 had been established in England alone. Medieval education came to be dominated by the Church, from the smallest class run by the parish priest to what were to become famous universities run by clergy.

The great explosion in the number of schools came, however, in the nineteenth century, with the Victorian zeal and earnestness for individual and social improvement. Church schools offering elementary education to local children founded often by the vicar and his wife were set up in towns and villages. I came to realize what a transformation such schools could make when I attended a service organized to mark the 150th anniversary of such a village school. As part of the celebrations the school and the local church had produced a small exhibition which included school books from the early days of the school and the contemporary parish registers of births, marriages and deaths. As I glanced through the marriage registers I noticed that after a certain date, what had earlier appeared as crosses had become signatures. Looking more closely I realized that the date when this happened was about ten years after the establishment of the village school. The ex-pupils were now literate, and if they were equipped to sign their names on marriage, they also had other options for their working lives undreamed of by their fathers and mothers.

One in five children in England receive their primary education in Church of England schools and the Church also has over 220 secondary schools and is involved in further and higher education, with most colleges having chaplains and innumerable lay Christians involved in teaching in both the Church and public sector. Other Christian denominations, particularly the Roman Catholic Church, also have a clear stake in education and now other faiths are following the Jewish pattern of establishing religious schools within the state system. The teaching ministry is one both valued and understood within religious circles, and I said as such in a 'Thought' given in July 1990.

WHO'D BE A TEACHER? 17 JULY 1990

Who'd be a teacher? Morale, we're told, is low, and with the latest government reshuffle it seems that being a teaching minister is hardly more secure than being a teacher. Who'd be a teacher. Well I would, for one. Indeed for much of my ministry I have been, combining the role of teacher with that of chaplain – teaching maths to hairdressers and farming students in rural Cambridgeshire; science to some pretty tough lads in a Kent Secondary Modern School; then for a long spell teaching electronics to students at new universities in Africa and Britain. Occasionally a face from the past stops me in the street or at a social gathering, 'You remember me, you taught me …' and I get a whole life story, a life story which I, for good or ill, had a hand in shaping.

Such influence brings both pain and joy to the teacher. Pain: what of the student who committed suicide? Did I give him too little attention? Joy: what of the day when I felt the hairs at the back of my head tingling with excitement as I began to get unexpected questions from a new student? It wasn't just that I couldn't answer the questions: it was that I'd never even thought of them, and I realized that I had a remarkable mathematician on my hands, and this from a student fresh from a school deep in the African bush.

Being a teacher is like being the manager of a football team: everybody else thinks that they could do the job better than you; and if teaching were merely passing on the treasures of the past and guarding the standards of society, perhaps everyone would be right. But a teacher has an allegiance to the future also, a future which is still unknown and unshaped, and realizing that future involves skill and risk and can't be too carefully prescribed. A teacher might stroke and polish the lamp of some agreed curriculum, but what the teacher aims to release is the genie of talent which will live and blossom way beyond the classroom.

The founders of the great religions were teachers who released new vision in whole communities. Certainly, according to the new piece of computer software which I've just purchased, 'teacher' was the title most often given to Jesus of Nazareth by the people of his day, for his words wove magic and lives were transformed as people saw and shared his vision of a world put right for God. It was a vision for which he lived and for which he was prepared to die. It was a vision he called upon others to share and make real, with one qualification: the teacher, he taught, first and foremost must be prepared to be the servant. Almost his last words to his disciples were these, 'You call me teacher and lord and you are right to do so. I have just washed your feet, you then should wash one another's feet.' Those who see things that way make the best teachers. Whether they get much thanks, whether they're religious or not, they discover that they're called to the ministry of teaching. There's no higher calling.

In the 'Thought' I touch upon the love of learning which is at the heart of all good education. For me, a poem which best encapsulates this comes from the pen of a writer, not usually regarded as being religious, D. H. Lawrence:

Thought, I love thought.
But not the juggling and twisting of already existing ideas.
I despise that self-important game.

Thought is the welling up of unknown life into consciousness,
Thought is the testing of statements on the touchstone of the
    conscience,
Thought is gazing on to the face of life, and reading what can be
    read,
Thought is pondering over experience, and coming to a conclusion.
Thought is not a trick, or an exercise, or a set of dodges,
Thought is a man in his wholeness wholly attending.

This love of learning can penetrate to the heart of virtually every subject on the curriculum because it involves both rigour and the freedom of speculation. It is to be found in the detailed study of scientific experimentation, in pouring over novels and manuscripts, in the contemplation and praise of a worshipping community. It is difficult to prescribe but students drink it in automatically from the best teachers. Most of my own pleading with politicians over the years has been to ask them to allow teachers to get on with their vocation without too much prescription or interference. My plea has mostly fallen upon deaf ears which is not too surprising as the following quote attributed (perhaps wrongly) to Petronius in the fifth century makes the same complaint:

> We trained hard ... but it seemed that every time we were beginning to form up into teams we would be reorganized. I was to learn later in life that we tend to meet any new situation by reorganizing; and a wonderful method it can be for creating the illusion of progress while producing confusion, inefficiency, and demoralization.

It was when watching a play by David Hare in 1992 that I suddenly realized what was at the heart of so much political interference in education. The play was modelled on a larger than life bishop, Mervyn Stockwood, Bishop of Southwark. Six years later I was myself to become Bishop of Southwark and began to know some of the other characters in the play. The heart of the play took place before the start of a service in the vestry of a church where an old college friend of the bishop was vicar. As the bishop puts on successive layer upon layer of exotic clothing he becomes more like a prelate and less like an old friend. The following 'Thought' describes what happened.

DON'T DO IT, MINISTER, 8 JANUARY 1992

In David Hare's play Racing Demon *there's a scene where a bishop is interviewing one of his vicars. The bishop wants to move the vicar because he feels that he's not sufficiently effective. The vicar and bishop had been at college together and so are speaking bluntly to one another. The vicar says something like this: 'Look, I really do understand. As a bishop you're surrounded by great problems and issues, most of which you can do nothing about. Then my little situation comes before you and it is possible for you to act there, and the temptation to do something positive in one area of your work, even if it's the wrong thing, must be overwhelming. But don't do it, Charlie – it's not fair.'*

I feel the same when I listen to the politicians bouncing around their latest ideas on educational reform. I really do understand. The world is in a great recession. A general election is around the corner. The Gulf War ended messily. The Soviet bloc has broken up and who knows whether utopia or fascism lies around the corner. All these are great issues and any politician must feel helpless and inadequate to deal with them. But then there's schools, and we all understand schools because we all went to school. The temptation to act decisively in one area of political life which we feel we understand is immense. But don't do it, Minister. Schoolteachers in the last few years have been overwhelmed with good ideas and initiatives from every political party, and they seem to me to be tired, shell shocked, unappreciated. No profession can cope with a management revolution, a curriculum revolution, an examination revolution, and a revolution in training, all in the space, it seems of two years – not if we want to get the best out of them. Continuous revolution was the hallmark of the discredited Maoist regime in Marxist

China. Continuous revolution is not necessarily a helpful hallmark of an educational system.

Jesus in Matthew's Gospel advises us not to worry overmuch about the speck of dust in our neighbour's eye when we have major problems in seeing straight because of the plank of wood sticking in our own eye. Of course we would like children to grow to maturity, civilized, knowledgeable, aware of their heritage and equipped to make their way in a changing world. But this is not a task for schools alone – it's a task that we all share. Personally I'm grateful that teachers do so well for our children in school. In the Church we need to rise to the challenge of coping with them fruitfully out of school hours and I suggest that others do the same.

The Bible speaks of people of faith being a pilgrim people. Our society is a community on the move into an unknown future. That fact needs to be faced bravely so that we can be prepared to live as a pilgrim people who don't have all the answers but who teach and learn from one another as we go, adults and children alike. Then, bishop or minister, Charlie wouldn't have to leap into taking unfair decisions, to take his mind off worrying about the future.

The basic message of the play was that a bishop has many insoluble problems arriving in his postbag every day. When a problem arrives which he is able to solve, then, he is under great temptation to do so, even if the solution is wrong or unjust, so that he can tell himself, 'Well at least I've taken one decision today.' 'Don't it Charlie,' his old friend says, 'it's not fair.'

Through the play I understood that something very similar goes on at the heart of government. Innumerable insoluble problems come the way of ministers, but, because we all went to school, when a question of education comes the way of a minister, the great temptation is to solve it, even though the answer is wrong, or better left alone.

A few days after delivering my 'Thought' I received a letter from a teacher in Leeds. She wrote that she had been listening to my 'Thought' on the car radio on the way to work and that she had had to pull into a lay-by because she was crying. The reason, she said, was because so much criticism comes the way of teachers, she had never expected someone publically to say anything supportive about them. That letter brought home to me just how low the morale of the teaching profession must have been in those days, and the tendency of new ministers of education of all political colours to make their mark by bringing in radical changes has not altered in 20 years. My message, 'Leave them alone, Minister', is still basically the same.

In those 20 years the political fashion has been, more and more, in education as in other areas of public life, to judge the worth of the project by measurable targets. A 'Thought' early in 1999 questioned this.

MEASURING, 15 JANUARY 1999

During the Vietnam War it is reported that the American Secretary for Defence, Robert McNamara, discovered that the army was using enemy body counts as the only criteria of the success of a mission, completely missing the point that the more people killed, the more intransigent the enemy became. He told his generals, 'We have to find a way of making the important measurable instead of making the measurable important.' But there lies the difficulty: how do you measure morale, commitment, patriotism?

Like the generals we usually settle for simply making important what we can measure, and that can distort our judgement. During the last week teachers' leaders, for example, were suggesting that the Ofsted measuring process in schools is detrimental to education, whilst medics and health workers were suggesting that the concentration on waiting lists was distorting the capacity of a hospital to respond to chronic or emergency health needs. The question is 'Are school league tables, or hospital waiting lists, any better a measure in the war against ignorance and disease than the Northern Vietnamese body counts were an indication that America was winning the war?'

But if it's a mistake to make the measurable important, because that distorts the whole process, the dilemma remains, 'How do you make the important measurable?', 'How do we measure good education or good health?' or 'How do we measure whether or not people will make good or even adequate parents?' For not to have any objective criteria leaves us prey to judgements merely being based on emotion or instinct, or habit, all of which can be equally suspect.

We get the same dilemma at the heart of the Bible. In the very last book of the Bible, St John meticulously spells out the dimensions of the heavenly city, 12,000 stadia long and wide it seems, with a wall 144 cubits high surrounding it. All very exact – and perhaps this was John's way of saying that the coming kingdom of God was no wish dream; it was to be solid and real. Yet St John was too wise and experienced to believe that the most important things can be measured. On his deathbed, as his disciples gathered around him for his last words, he is reported as saying, 'Little children, love one another.' 'Yes, yes,' they replied, 'but you've said that to us before.' 'Little children, love one another,' the saint repeated, 'there is nothing else to say.' And with that he died, leaving us with the dilemma that body counts, league tables, waiting lists and even city walls can be measured, but how do you measure peace, and justice and love, and should you try?

Another tendency in recent times has been to insist that good education results in effective practical results, but it has equally been argued that an educational system isn't worth a great deal if it teaches young people how to make a living yet doesn't teach them how to make a life. Any teacher knows that it is possible to store facts galore into a student's mind and still leave the student entirely uneducated.

Yet, given all of this in schools in recent years subjects not regarded as being of a practical nature – such as classical languages, art, music, religious studies – have had to struggle to justify their place on the curriculum, and 'pure' rather than 'applied' research has found it difficult to find public funding. The problem is that it is not always easy to foresee what will bring practical results. Albert Einstein was a rather average student but later claimed that imagination was more important than knowledge. 'Knowledge is limited,' he wrote, 'imagination encircles the world.' The great J. J. Thomson, the inventor of the electron, would have agreed with him. He once said that if government policy had been operating in the Stone Age today we would have wonderful stone axes but no one would have discovered metals. Werner von Braun, the father of the rockets which produced the moon landing, said 'Basic research is doing what I am doing when I don't know what I am doing.' How do you measure that?

There is some merit in the criticism that education pure and simple can take the form of some ivory tower existence which does nothing to prepare its students for the realities of later life. The late Alistair Cooke in one of his 'Letters from America' spoke of interviewing a heavyweight boxing champion in his dressing room just after the champ had knocked out his opponent. 'What do you think of your opponent,' he asked him. The champ reflected, 'He's a fine boxer. He's a boxer who thinks, and while he's in the ring there thinking, I go in and batter his brains out, because thinking ain't real and it's reality that counts.'

Well, thinking is real, of course, but it's not the whole of reality and a school or college educating its pupils properly will want to prepare them for a world that all too easily will batter their brains out. Those teaching, or learning in urban schools in Britain know only too well how easily this can happen. I presented this 'Thought' in December 2000 shortly after the stabbing to death of the 10-year-old Damilola Taylor in the stairwell of a block of flats in Peckham, south London.

PECKHAM, 4 DECEMBER 2000

It's been a pretty devastating week for the people of Peckham. Their sympathy for young Damilola Taylor's parents and family is very real but local folk are getting a little tired of their estate being portrayed day after day as some sort of hell hole. Meanwhile the press continue to besiege Damilola's school, looking for stories from pupils and staff alike. But the truth is that urban streets are dangerous, and they're dangerous for one particular group of people – teenage boys and young men. They make up a large proportion of perpetrators of violent crime, but they are also a large proportion of the victims. Partly there's nothing new in this. From the time of West Side Story, *through the phase of rockers and skinheads, teenage boys have always spent a great deal of time hanging about urban streets in groups, carving out their patch of territory, fighting with other groups who dared to come near or who were different in some way from themselves. Meanwhile, older people or young children went on their way sublimely ignorant of this sub-plot in their local community.*

What is different today? The difference is that many teenage boys are carrying knives. They'll tell you that its for their own protection, but there's a thin line between protection and provocation. The difference is – drugs. Drugs and violence go together, as people commit crimes to get the money to feed their habit, or fight to protect their drug-pushing patch. The difference is that there are lots of teenage boys hanging about the streets rather than in school. There are 18,000 pupils excluded from school at present, or to put it in language we understand, suspended or expelled. Why? Because it's becoming increasingly difficult to handle disruptive pupils in schools without damaging the academic results of the other pupils, and in a world where academic league tables are all, and where there's no credit given for the far more difficult task of handling and civilizing angry young people, out the troublemakers must go – to the tender care of the streets.

Damilola Taylor's murder has made the invisible, visible, because, unusually it's a 10-year-old boy who is the victim. If it had been a 16 or 17 year old I doubt whether we'd have heard of it because, sadly, it's not unusual for boys of that age to get wounded or even killed on our urban streets. Some £240 million is being spent rebuilding Peckham. There are far worse places to live. Urban poverty is being tackled there quite successfully. But the real challenge in Peckham and elsewhere is the moral poverty of sin and self. In a week or two the media will have departed, but the Churches and the schools will still be there, fighting for goodness and grace in a world which devalues both. But then that's the world we've created.

Brains can be battered out in more subtle ways than in the violence of urban streets. We are all very susceptible and are easily influenced by the views and attitudes of those around us. That is why a culture of a school is as important as its curriculum. The aim is to produce a humane school community respecting religious and cultural differences but looking to common ethical standards where as well as appreciating and teaching a love of learning, students have the opportunity to explore their own beliefs and their response to fundamental questions.

A few years ago I was talking to the chair of governors of a large comprehensive school in Brent. It wasn't a Church school but he told me that all the children took GCSE exams in religious studies. 'I didn't realize that it was so popular with students,' I said. 'It's isn't popular with them,' he replied, 'but it's popular with their parents. Religion means standards, and that's what every parent wants from a school.' I suddenly realized that this is the reason why Church schools are so popular with parents. They might not be in any way religious themselves, but they associate religion with standards, standards of behaviour and achievement, and, rightly or wrongly, Church schools benefit from this association, and, of course, once a culture of behaviour and achievement is set, it is more easy to maintain it. The opposite is also true. In June 2009 I presented a 'Thought' on the 'Nocebo Effect'.

NOCEBO, 16 JUNE 2009

Some years ago when I was lecturing at a university in Central Africa we had a sophisticated student of electronics going totally to pieces before his final examination because he believed that someone in his home village had put a destructive spell on him. According to a recent article in a scientific magazine such cases aren't confined to rural Africa. We're all very familiar with the placebo effect, a person's belief, for example, that medicine will do good, even if it has no active ingredients in it whatsoever, but apparently scientists are discovering that the opposite effect, the nocebo effect can be quite as powerful. A case is reported of a young man, after splitting up with his girlfriend, taking a bottleful of pills. Then he regretted it and headed for the hospital where he collapsed. Four hours later, having received four litres of saline and showing no improvement, a doctor arrived and revealed that the patient had in fact been in a control group and, unknown to him, the pills he'd taken were harmless. When given this good news, within 15 minutes he was fully alert with his blood pressure returned to normal.

The nocebo effect can, of course, be extremely dangerous; a misdi-agnosis from an authoritative doctor indicating a fatal illness, with everyone then starting to act on that belief, can be a self-fulfilling prophecy with the person dying even though the original condition was in fact benign. The nocebo effect may also affect the behaviour of large groups. Reported symptoms in some can trigger similar mass effect in others. A few years ago 800 children in Jordan apparently suffered side effects after a vaccination and over 120 of them were admitted to hospital, but after extensive tests no problem whatsoever could be found with the vaccine.

Well it would seem that we have plenty to worry about at the present time. Apart from anxieties in our personal lives, the world might well see a swine flu pandemic in the autumn. The repercussions of the financial crunch, some of them unpredictable, will affect us for several years to come. The lack of confidence in political life might have serious constitutional consequences. With all of this it would be easy to become immobilized with fear. The nocebo effect could kick in in abundance. But it's not inevitable. In similar times, President Franklin D. Roosevelt told the American people 'The only thing that we have to fear is fear itself,' and on the basis of that philosophy began to rebuild the world. Two thousand years ago, a biblical writer wrote an even more powerful message: 'Perfect love casts out fear.' It has been claimed that it was this powerful message which combated the immobilizing fear of witch-craft which was the reason why Christianity swept though Africa as a

liberating force and remains the majority faith of that continent. It's
worth trying in our own lives.

If Church schools are well placed to combat the nocebo effect by having
a faith ethos which permeates the total life of the school and, at its best,
communicates the message that every child is valuable with a unique
set of gifts which the school aims to uncover and develop, we also have
to admit that there are potential dangers in such schools being major
players in the state educational system. When most elementary schools
were Church of England schools there was no question of Church
schools being divisive through their selection procedures, for there was
a place for every local child.

Things became more complicated after the 1944 Education Act and
the raising of the school leaving age. The Church of England did not
attempt to build sufficient secondary schools to provide a place for every
pupil leaving one of its Church primary schools. The Roman Catholic
Church did provide such places and saw the education of children from
Roman Catholic homes as a major responsibility and priority in its
overall ministry.

The Church of England, with its relatively fewer, but extremely
popular, secondary schools, found that most were oversubscribed. The
Church of England could not at secondary level offer a place in a Church
school for every child from the community who wanted a place and
selection procedures usually based on the Church connection of the
parents became the norm. This had all kinds of implications on local
Church life, with the temptation for 'nominal Christians' to attend their
local church until their child had a secure place in the Church school.
Many clergy and lay people were also uncomfortable that, with white
English parents being disproportionately at least nominally Christians,
many Church secondary schools did not reflect the ethnic make-up of
the surrounding community. In parts of inner city London, however,
with Afro-Caribbean parents being predominately Christian, Church
secondary schools disproportionately favoured the admission of their

children and have proved to be a great springboard of educational opportunity for them.

There are those who, looking at the not overhappy record of Church schools in Northern Ireland, adding to sectarian divisions, feel that faith schools have no place in a modern Britain of many faiths and none. It is the case, of course, that the study of religions other than Christianity is developed in Church schools with more rigour than in most state schools but certainly there can be no argument that if Church schools receive state funding, as they do particularly in salary support, then other faiths should be afforded a similar opportunity. To develop their own schools, Jewish schools have been a valued part of the education spectrum for decades and there is no reason why schools from other major world faiths should not now join them, provided that the curriculum and school discipline conform to national standards.

With non-religious state schools there is also the anxiety that in the periodic revolution in national educational policy, religious studies runs the risk of being downgraded or even disappearing from the curriculum. This would be a great loss. It used to be thought that religion was a thing of the past and could take its place in history. Now, it has become clear that there is no way of understanding adequately the hopes, aspirations and fears of people around the globe without an understanding of religion. Religious education at its best can provide a bridge between the rigour and discipline of good intellectual endeavour and the realities of the world of today and tomorrow. In particular it has the structure and ability to ask the question 'What is right behaviour in the future world which is coming at us so rapidly?' Two events in May 1998 brought the question to the forefront of my mind and occasioned the 'Thought' 'Future Shock'.

FUTURE SHOCK, 13 MAY 1998

Alvin Toffler some 20 years ago brought out a book entitled Future Shock. *A shiver of future shock touched me yesterday as two news items were reported. The Indian prime minister announced with some pride that India had tested three nuclear weapons. Now a country like ours which has had nuclear weapons for 50 years or more is in no position to take a high moral tone, but my reaction was one of deep sadness that a nation founded in modern times on the great moral authority of Gandhi and his methodology of non-violent action should now so publicly see its security in weapons of mass destruction. If India isn't strong enough to resist this temptation then what nation will? Future shock – when every nation has its nuclear or biological arsenal.*

And biology was the second news story which troubled me. The European Parliament was deciding whether or not commercial companies could patent discoveries regarding strands of DNA. I have a background in science and hence know the excitement of scientific research where facts fall into place within the prediction of a successful hypothesis. Usually I'm on the side of scientific freedom (as I believe, on balance, that scientists can be trusted to act responsibly). But when large sums of money are involved then scientific principles can be bent in the interests of commercial gain, and when genetic engineering is the science then the end result just might be – future shock.

As we learn more about the internal workings of our universe and the scientific laws which govern it, theologians have come also to a new understanding about the workings of God. They see God creating a universe with the energy, ability and freedom to make itself. And what that universe has thrown up is creatures like ourselves: visionary dreamers, selfish killers, decent citizens. Over thousands of years the moral laws were formulated to enable civilized life to develop. The great religions had their part to play in this great civilizing endeavour. But we now live in a different world. In the last century there has been a tremendous step forward in scientific understanding and technological development, yet our morality is still that of the small town and village, and it just isn't adequate to deal with some of the decisions now facing us.

We are now, I believe, scientific geniuses and moral pygmies. And that's dangerous when we have the technological capacity to destroy ourselves. The challenge for the coming millennium is to give as much priority to developing the moral guidelines for life in a volatile high-tech global village as we do to technological research and development. There may not be money in such morality, we may not be able to patent it – but it might be a matter of life or death.

Handling the practice of religion is not easy in most schools and yet religion for most people in most parts of the world is near the heartbeat of their lives. Valiant efforts in school are made to study the world religions in a fair and objective way, but this rather misses the point: it is like studying football through diagrams on a blackboard, without ever going onto the field and playing a game. In 1999 as part of the preparations for the new millennium that Archbishop of Canterbury invited each of the 44 dioceses in England to send its bishop accompanied by up to a hundred teenagers to a gathering in the extensive gardens of Lambeth Palace. Called 'The Time of Our Lives', it was an illuminating occasion with young and old alike enjoying the sunshine and the company and together taking in different experiences. I described it in a 'Thought' presented the following week.

TIME OF OUR LIVES, 4 MAY 1999

As a child one of the books on my bedside bookcase was called Adventure Stories for Boys *and amongst its heroes were Irving and Mallory who bravely went to their death in 1924 trying to be the first people on earth to reach the summit of Mount Everest. Yesterday it was reported that the body of George Mallory, wearing his tweed jacket and leather shoes, had been discovered a thousand feet or so below the summit. To Mallory, climbing Everest wasn't only a challenge of physical endurance – it was a mystical quest, for he spoke of Everest in terms of awe and wonder. He would well have appreciated the experience of a later expedition who had made excellent progress during the first five days of the climb. On the sixth day the leader emerged from his tent keen on making an early start, only to discover that the Sherpas had no intention of climbing that day. 'No,' said the head Sherpa, 'Our bodies have climbed up high during the past five days; now we rest so that our souls can catch up.'*

Resting so that our souls can catch up is one of the benefits of a bank-holiday weekend to those of us who lead frantic lives. I don't know how you spent your weekend, but I was amongst the 59 bishops who had a busman's holiday. We met in the gardens of Lambeth Palace to help give some three and a half thousand young Christians, gathered from every part of England, what was called 'The Time of Our Lives'. The archbishop had organized the event to give young Christians the sense of being part of something much bigger than the life of their local church. There were concerts and discos; indeed, my ears are still ringing with the sound of the music. There were workshops on issues such as world debt, the coming new millennium, care for the globe. There was magnificent worship of all traditions in the abbey and cathedrals.

But what struck me was something quite different. In the midst of a crazy garden party on Saturday afternoon, with wild music and games, dotted around Lambeth Palace gardens were figures who at first I took to be painted statues. But they weren't – they were mime artists, sitting utterly still in the midst of all the activity. And gradually, gradually, young people began to gather around them and sit and share their stillness – islands of tranquillity in the heart of a vibrant world. And so in a weekend of wild music, new friendships, endless discussion, high idealism, lack of sleep, sitting quietly in Lambeth garden in quiet meditation, our souls had a chance to catch up with our restless bodies and minds. I need more moments like that in my life; perhaps you do, too.

I referred earlier to religious education providing a bridge between good intellectual endeavour and the 'realities of the world of today and tomorrow'. I suspect, however, that religion at its best has far more than this to offer as young and old go into the future. The film *The Man of La Mancha* is based on Cervantes' story of Don Quixote. The opening scene of the film is set in the dungeons of a castle in Spain during the time of the Inquisition. A varied company of prisoners await the torment of examination. One is a hard-headed young doctor, very much a modern man. He is irritated by the fact that a fellow prisoner, a poet, is writing poetry whilst he waits. 'How can you write poetry in a place like this?' he challenges. 'Poets spin nonsense out of nothing, blurring men's eyes to reality.' 'Exactly!' the poet replies. 'Reality is a stone prison crushing the human spirit. Poetry demands imagination, and with imagination you may discover a dream.' The doctor will not leave it there, however. 'A man has to come to terms with life as it is,' he asserts. 'Life as it is,' reflects the poet, ' I've lived for over forty years and I've seen life as it is – pain, misery, cruelty beyond belief. I've heard all the voices of God's noblest creatures – moans from bundles of filth in the street. I've been a soldier and a slave. I've seen my comrades fall in battle or die more slowly under the lash. These were men who saw life as it is but they died despairing. No glory, no brave last words, only their eyes filled with confusion, questioning "Why?" I do not think that they were questioning why they were dying, but why they had ever lived. When life itself seems lunatic. Who knows where madness lies? Perhaps to be too practical is madness. To surrender dreams, this may be madness. To seek treasure where there is only trash. Too much sanity may be madness. And maddest of all – to see life as it is and not as it should be.'

Education at its best must include both seeing and coping with life as it is whilst raising the vision of life as it should be. Such education sees every child and the adult the child will become as being uniquely valuable. It realizes that children must be given the skills to make their own way in the world. But the 'tick box' of gaining desirable skills should not block out the sense of wonder and respect for the world and its future, nor the desire to work together to help make that world a better place for all.

Whilst a minority of teenagers in Britain today will have a formal religious belief, the element of global neighbourliness is very much part of their concern. This shows itself both in a desire to show a care for the environment and study the effects of global warming, particularly on the vulnerable parts of the globe and as a sense of solidarity with people their age living in such places. There are projects which help hook the imagination of young people here which can be of great value to young people in Africa, for example. I drew attention to one such project, 'Give One, Get One Computers' in a 'Thought' in 2007.

GIVE ONE, GET ONE COMPUTERS, 25 SEPTEMBER 2007

Back in the early 1970s I was both university chaplain and a lecturer in electronics at the University of Zambia. By one of those surprises which characterize African development, we were donated a state-of-the-art research computer and the air-conditioned lab to house it. The lab was soon crowded as air conditioning was rare in tropical Africa, but only a few of us mastered the use of the computer. But for those of us who did, at a time when computer use in Western universities was being allocated in ten-minutes slots, we had hours of computing time available. We did some useful research but in no way did it impact upon the lives of ordinary Zambians.

But a computing project which just might, caught my eye yesterday. It's called the G1G1 scheme, producing a laptop designed to be used by children in rural villages in the least developed countries around the globe. It has no moving parts, has a sunlight readable display, can be powered by solar, foot-pump or pull-string power, and is housed in a waterproof case. The software is as imaginative as the machine itself, with universal pictorial icons giving instant access to a range of educational programmes.

All of this costs at present a little less than £100 but the aim is to bring the price down to £50 per unit. This is still beyond the pocket of most rural people in places such as Africa, Cambodia and Afghanistan, and this is where the G1G1 kicks in. G1G1 is short for 'give one, get one' and the plan will allow, at the moment, United States residents to purchase two laptops for $400. One will be sent to the buyer whilst a child in the developing world will receive the second machine. This seems to me to be a creative combination of technological innovation, grass-root *rural development, and our natural instinct not to miss a bargain. Supermarkets more usually exploit the latter instinct by offering 'buy one, get one free'. It's good to see the same technique being used, not for selfish reasons, but for reasons of altruism in the 'give one, get one' project.*

A much loved prayer asks that by God's holy inspiration we may think those things that are good, and by his merciful guiding may perform the same. A $100-computer for rural children would have been beyond the imagining of the writers of that prayer, but the One Laptop Per Child project fits the sentiment: good thoughts have designed, developed and produced a machine and a 'give one, get one' strategy that could have a transforming effect on countless lives. Just for once, we might have got something right in development.

The nurturing of this sense of global neighbourliness in an otherwise competitive world should be, and is, at the heart of a good education, but both the competitive and the cooperative instincts lie deep within the human psyche and perhaps the world is best served when both can be utilized and harnessed. It is often in school life outside the classroom that this can best be demonstrated and developed. In a 'Thought' presented in 2010 I related the saga of the end of a cross-country race at a certain school.

SCHOOL SPORT, 7 DECEMBER 2010

The funding of competitive sports in schools has risen up the political agenda amid uncertainty over the future of school sports partnerships. The government has indicated that it's reviewing its proposals to bring direct funding to an end following an outcry from many leading athletes. I hope that there's a good outcome.

At present I'm spending two terms as a bishop in residence at a large boarding school and I'm getting some idea of just how important compulsory sport is to its common life. At its most basic, if teenage boys and girls aren't playing sport several afternoons a week then they have plenty of unused energy; perhaps that's why many sports were invented in English public schools. Certainly, with the sports pitches frozen this last week, the staff in the boarding houses had their hands full in the evening calming down overlively youngsters. But there's more to compulsory school sport than soaking up energy. The good players will always find their way into representative teams, but the mediocre performers might have just as much fun from participating but wouldn't get the opportunity unless every pupil is encouraged to have a go.

Soon after the start of term I was standing at the door of one of the houses at teatime just as the new pupils were staggering in from their first cross-country run. A sixth former was greeting them. 'How did you do?' he asked each boy. 'Where did you come?' 'Eighth,' said the first arrival. 'Oh, well done, well done.' 'Seventeenth,' said the next. 'Oh, well done, well done.' Then came the next arrival, some time later. 'Where did you come?' 'Thirty-sixth.' 'Oh, well done, well done,' said the sixth former, 'Do you know, coming thirty-sixth rather than thirty-seventh might have made all the difference to whether or not our house wins the cup?' And the young lad went in, walking tall. If that's not an example of character building for both boys, I don't know what is.

I think I now understand rather better why St Paul the apostle chose the runners in the Olympic games of his day as models for character building in the Christian life. He says that in a race all the runners run but only one gets the prize, a laurel crown. But everyone who competes has to go into strict training. And if runners do that for a crown that won't last, how serious his followers should be in their journey of faith to a crown that lasts for ever. Our own London Olympics will, of course, soon be with us. Now, surely, is the time to make certain that children in all our schools get the chance to experience the fun and pride of competitive sport, and that we all take seriously our journeying together for the common good, even if we do come in thirty-sixth.

Cardinal Newman once said that education must be good and useful, and although the useful is not always good, the good is always useful.

When working to establish a new university in Ireland in the nineteenth century he summed up what insight a religious viewpoint might bring to the vital arena of education. 'If then a practical end must be assigned to a university course, I say it is that of training good members of society. Its art is the art of social life, and its end is fitness for the world … It is the education which gives a man a clear conscious view of his own opinion and judgements, a truth in developing them, an eloquence in expressing them, and a force in urging them.' The early chapters in this book illustrate that sort of education or the lack of it as we have wrestled with some of the other important issues of the day.

The fundamental question is whether we see childhood as a preparation for adult life or as a valuable experience in itself which will not come again. If it is the latter, we will not have done right by future generations of children if we teach them how to make a living but do not teach them how to make a life. The great religious teacher Jesus of Nazareth went even further than this, saying to adults, 'Unless you become as little children, you will not see the Kingdom of Heaven.' In his upside down world, then, childhood is not a preparation for adulthood – it is an insight into ways and wisdoms which adults have forgotten. Albert Einstein, when asked how he had come to make some of his remarkable breakthroughs in science, said, 'I continued to ask the questions that children ask.' Perhaps there lies the clue to true education.

9

Religion and Religion

The previous chapters have attempted to examine the effect of religion in the marketplace and the way it reflects upon and affects issues in public life. This chapter will attempt to turn the spotlight upon religion itself, and organized religion in particular, because religion is not problem-free and in organized religion we get all the stresses and strains of other human groups. I will try to focus upon where the shoe is pinching rather then telling uplifting stories. For some adherents their religion provides a reliable backcloth to their lives, a source of comfort and strength in times of trouble, but is not in the forefront of their concern in the normal business of getting on with their lives. For others their religion is the driving force for all they think or do. Through it they may well pioneer ways forward through obstacles others would find daunting, they may equally with passion and commitment drive down destructive blind alleys. Because of this, religion can be a servant of, or a threat to, the common good.

In human reasoning there is always the danger of stringing a number of beliefs together and coming to a false conclusion. Each of the beliefs in themselves might be good or harmless, but strung together the result might be destructive. It is common in all walks of life to follow the persuasive but illogical argument. 'Something must the done. This is something. Therefore this must be done.' Equally, on 9/11 we saw a religious argument which perhaps went something like this: 'Allah is great. True Muslims seek to do his will. When the community is under threat it must be protected'. There is a good and legitimate argument for each one of those pearls of belief. But when a further, less well accepted, adage is added, 'to kill to protect the community is not a sin but a duty', and the conclusion is reached, 'therefore the Twin Towers must be destroyed', we have a total string of argument which is both erroneous and destructive. The problem is that to the young men in the planes and those who supported them the string comes as a total package and is believed as fervently as any one of the individual pearls of belief.

This religious dynamic is not confined to Islam. We saw it operating in a similar way at Waco in the United States in 1993. Here the argument ran, 'God is good and must be obeyed. The Church exists in community. The Church community needs a godly leader. The leader should be followed and obeyed. A good Christian should be prepared to lay down his or her life for the faith. Therefore, if the leader tells you to, you should die together.' Again, many of those pearls of faith would be accepted by many Christians although those of a more liberal persuasion would begin to get uncomfortable with the notion of obeying a leader, however wise and good. But strung together as a total, illogical, string of faith there is always the danger of a Waco. The Waco disaster was the product of a tightly-knit religious sect under the leadership of a charismatic leader, David Koresh. For 50 days they fought off investigating federal agents before 76 of them, including 20 children, were killed in a fire.

WACO, 20 APRIL 1993

We're all shocked by the news coming out of Waco – I'm not sure whether a Churchman or a psychiatrist should be attempting to offer a thought for the day after such a tragic event. Certainly the deaths of some 80 people in the circumstances of a religious community shows the shadow side of religion – what can be the outcome when individuals give their lives into the hands of a charismatic religious leader who offers certainty and demands mindless obedience.

How is it that people can find themselves in such a situation? Well, if you pound people hard enough with certainty when they're feeling vulnerable under the pressures of life; if you offer them instant family when their lives are poor in friendship; if you offer them a message which

*makes meaning of life, when their lives are confused and problematical;
if you offer them a special task – to spread the groups' gospel when their
work is dull or meaningless, or they can find no work to do; if you offer
them clear leadership when they can find no one to admire believe in or
follow in their world or Church; if you offer all this, together with intoxi-
cating, mind-numbing worship – then you're offering a powerful package
which many people will buy.*

*The psychological danger of doing so is obvious to us in the tragic
events of the last 12 hours. And perhaps it is right for a Churchman to
say it. It is a sad truth that mystical insight and mad illusion seem to
lie close together in the human psyche. The great religions have always
known this and so have their checks and balances through worship and
prayer so that people can get in touch with the reality of God without
destroying themselves in the process. A religion can and should bring
holiness and goodness to the lives of its followers, but the religious
impulse, out of control, can become a dangerous drug, and in the hands
of an unscrupulous leader it can be a menace.*

*The psychological danger is obvious then, but there is an equally real
theological danger. I believe that the lust for certainty is the original
human sin. In the story in Genesis the forbidden fruit in the garden
which archetypal humans were forbidden to eat was from the tree of the
knowledge of good and evil. Eat it and you would be like gods. Eat it and
you would have certainty – eat it and everything would become clear.
A religious or political leader offering the fruit of certainty will always
have followers, who sometimes will follow him or her to their deaths.
I'm disturbed by those having terrible doubts, but I'm often even more
disturbed by those having terrible certainty.*

*For true religion doesn't offer certainty of this sort. It offers faith.
It offers a thoughtful walk with God. It offers a way of living in peace
without certainty. This morning I'm both sad and angry. I'm sad for
those poor people who have gone to their deaths and for their families
who grieve for them, and I'm angry that pseudo-religion has done this
to them. It makes me deeply ashamed.*

In this Waco 'Thought' I point to the 'Lust for Certainty' as being at the heart of the disaster. In a shaky world the desire for certainty is natural but a religion offering it is on dangerous grounds for this 'certainty' once embraced will be defended ferociously, particularly if the adherents' faith in it is beginning to wobble. Authentic religious faith is, in fact, faith and not certainty.

The Waco tragedy to some extent had been prefigured by the mass suicide at Jonestown in Guyana in November 1978. The Jonestown cult had been founded in 1955 by James Warren Jones and grew rapidly. He persuaded many of his Indianapolis congregation in 1977 to join him in building a new isolated community in a South American jungle. Relatives of some of the cult members grew concerned that they were being brainwashed and following a visit by Congressman Ryan, he and four others were shot by Jones's guards. Some members of Ryan's party escaped, however, and on hearing this Jones persuaded over 900 of his followers to drink cyanide, whilst he apparently shot himself in the head.

Waco and Jonestown seem to be extreme manifestations of the tendency in some versions of Protestant Christianity to sell religion as a desirable product. Churches of this type have seen successful growth both in the US and in the suburbs of Britain but it is a competitive world and their ministers have to demonstrate that what they have to offer is more sound than that on offer in the congregation across town. All too often the approach is to so convince the hearer of their sin and hopeless state, that the following offer of salvation through belief comes as wonderful news. The problem is that no other message is offered; the need for the believer to broaden and deepen faith, the need for the faith to be related to the ills of the world and tackle peace and justice issues, all these are ignored or neglected and the same narrow sermon is preached again and again with increased passion and conviction. I raised questions about this approach in a 'Thought' of March 1990, 'Selling Religion'.

SELLING RELIGION, 3 MARCH 1990

'A house-going vicar means a church-going people'. That always used to be the advice given to young clergy, meaning that if the vicar worked hard and visited his many parishioners in their homes, they would repay the compliment and come to his church. It's not always such good advice today when more often than not, both partners in a marriage are working during the day and are tired at night after their journey home. They don't want to see anybody, not even their friendly local vicar.

If our conscientious vicar does want to meet his parishioners, he could do worse than visit his local supermarket on a Saturday morning. This is the new place of community. It's certainly where my wife and I, living busy lives, renew our acquaintance with each other, and judging by the crowds all around, Saturday morning supermarket shopping is a popular family outing.

Of course once inside the supermarket it's not always easy to keep a grip on spending. 'Nothing is cheap if you don't need it,' my mother used to say, but the advertisers are expert at persuading us that we do need their product, and that we should buy it immediately whilst this week's offer lasts – six bars of chocolate for the price of five – who can resist? But the advertisers are more creative than that. They not infrequently inform us that their particular product is the answer to a problem which we didn't even know that we had. For example, we used to think that all we needed to worry about was whether our washing powder produced a clean wash, whereas now we're told that we should worry about whether our clean washing has a scent of spring about it.

Religion is not infrequently sold on the basis of being the answer to problems which we didn't know we had, and no doubt before long we'll be being battered by religious adverts through satellite TV convincing us that, although we didn't know it, we're in a terrible mess, and offering religious solutions guaranteed to wash us spiritually whiter than white and remove all those nasty human smells.

I've never been too happy with religious teaching which tries to open people's eyes to sin and damnation before offering them hope and salvation. That teaching can so easily lead to despair and disaster because, once having been convinced of the bad news, some folk find it difficult to believe the good. They neurotically go sniffing out the sin in themselves and others for the rest of their lives, whereas the Bible talks as much about human rightness as wrongness and Jesus was as likely to meet people in their joy and fun as in their pain and guilt.

Certainly I want people to believe in God, but I want people to believe not out of fear or despair, but because they've glimpsed something of the wonder of God, realize that a walk with God brings life in abundance here and now, and find in their local church a gracious and welcoming community. That's what I want, but meanwhile – see you in the supermarket contemplating the soap powders.

The heart of this 'Thought' is my general belief that salvation through fear is not at the heart of the good news of the Christian gospel What is at its heart is the abundant goodness and grace of God which overcomes fear and faithlessness. In the gospel stories we see Jesus Christ preaching and showing both grace and challenge and with different individuals they come in a different order. The important thing to note is that both are part of the package of good news.

I returned to the subject of supermarkets in a 'Thought' delivered in April 1999. It was virtually the only 'Thought' which I have presented which seemed to stir the passions of one of the *Today* presenters who followed me out of the studio and said, 'Do you mean to say that bishops do their own shopping!' It just shows what cocooned lives we live if broadcasters still believe that bishops are surrounded by servants: those days are long gone.

SUPERMARKETESE, 13 APRIL 1999

Supermarkets have been under the spotlight recently. Over the weekend the first wedding in a supermarket took place, perhaps a logical development of supermarkets being the secular cathedrals of our age. Then there's an investigation going on as to whether supermarkets are misusing their massive presence in the marketplace to disadvantage producers and consumers alike. And with anxieties surrounding genetically modified crops, questions are being asked about the labelling of supermarket products.

Well, it seems to me that even without GM complications labelling in supermarkets is not straightforward. I only do the basic shopping in our household – things like dog meat, washing powder, cereals, etc. – but I've noticed that with the more sophisticated stuff – meat and the like – there's a certain language of supermarketese which needs to be interpreted. 'Value for money' means affordable but very basic; 'premium' means expensive;'luxury' means very expensive; and 'connoisseur' means way beyond the Butler budget. It's okay once you've learned the language.

But of course my ministry takes me around an awful lot of local churches, and I realize that a similar task of interpretation needs to be going on there, too. 'Traditional' means we don't want a woman vicar. 'Forward looking' means we do want a woman vicar. 'Biblical' means we take the biblical teaching on personal morality very seriously. 'Prophetic' means we take the biblical teaching on social justice very seriously. 'Traditional worship' means Book of Common Prayer and we don't like modern hymns. 'All age worship' means children friendly words, music and drama so even adults might be able to understand the sermon. As with supermarkets, it's all very straightforward once you can break the language code.

The language of a Pentecostal church in Brentwood got it into trouble over the weekend. Apparently the Advertising Standards Authority disapproved of its newspaper advertisement claiming that a particular man had been completely cured of some infirmity during one of its services. Healing claims are notoriously sensitive. Healing does take place in hospital wards and churches, occasionally when the prognosis seems dire, but it's not automatic, and there's no guarantee, however firmly a person might believe, for otherwise how can we explain a God of love healing one person and leaving another faith-filled individual to die in agony. We don't need the Advertising Standards Authority to tell us that that doesn't add up.

But the Easter message is not 'Come to Church and we guarantee healing.' The Easter message is, that despite pain and suffering, despite disappointment and loss, despite Kosovo and cancer, and yes, despite the certainty of our own coming death, with God new life is always possible and so no world is unsaveable and no life is unliveable.

One of the several themes in this 'Thought' is the language describing the various strands of Church life even in the single denomination of the Church of England. Since the Reformation this Church has been 'Catholic and Reformed' and so it has both the Catholic and Protestant traditions within it, sometimes in quite extreme forms. But in addition it has a long-standing liberal strand which believes that God has things to say to the Church through developments in the world and is very influenced, for example, by the earlier struggle against apartheid or the civil rights movement in the US or human rights issues today. Then there is the central tradition often found in rural churches with a deep love of the Book of Common Prayer and the King James Bible and a general concern for things to be done with decency. And each of the strands have their 'keenies' wishing to fight their corner with passion and enthusiasm as well as their more quiet adherents. At its best the Church of England is a Church of thoughtful holiness; at its worst there is argumentative mayhem.

It may be instructive to follow through the two most divisive issues in the Church of England in recent times: the ordination of women as priests and bishops, and the question of gay people and clergy in the Church. A 'Thought' of January 1993 was given shortly after the General Synod had taken the decision that women could be ordained as priests, and arguments had started concerning how those who would find it difficult to accept their ministry might find protection. The wounds in the body of the Church which later widened were beginning to appear.

EROS, 17 JANUARY 1993

Piccadilly Circus is without a focal point at present. Two overenthusiastic revellers in October swung from the wings of the statue of Eros causing the leg upon which it balances to fracture. The statue is now in a workshop in Telford being repaired. The restorers report that Eros can go back if its leg is strengthened but they suggest that a better solution is for the original of Eros to be sent to a museum. A replica could then be cast and stand in Piccadilly circus in pristine glory. Westminster City Council is not convinced. The Council insists that Eros is a symbol of London and the original must be returned, cracks and all. And quite right, too.

The House of Bishops of the Church of England was faced with a similar dilemma last week. Since the decision of the General Synod last November to ordain women as priests many people have been swinging from the wings of the Church, bending it this way and that. And the Church bears scars from all that pressure, indeed some feared that it was cracked beyond repair. The bishops were faced with two ways forward. One was to cast something quite new – a kind of a Church within a Church – where those opposed to the ordination of women could have their own life and structures in pristine purity. But despite its attraction the bishops did not go for this, and neither were they prepared to see the Church of England consigned to some archaic museum of past glory.

No, they took the Church as it is, fractured and wounded in a cause that the majority of its members have demonstrated that they want, the ordination of women to the priesthood. And the bishops planned how they might restore and strengthen the structure through new supports extending their own ministry of pastoral and sacramental care, whilst keeping the integrity of the Church intact.

Eros of course, is a statue dedicated to love and I believe that such a statue should contain wounds and cracks because those of us who love know only too well that joy rarely comes without some pain. The Church also is dedicated to love: the generous self-giving love which was shown most vividly in the life of Jesus of Nazareth and described most movingly by one of his followers, St Paul. In Paul's words, that love is patient and kind. It does not insist on its own way. It does not rejoice at wrong, but rejoices in the right. Such love bears all things, believes all things, hopes all things, endures all things. A Church dedicated to that sort of love is going to be wounded from time to time and the worth of its witness is to be found in how it seeks to bind up its wounds and strengthen its body without turning aside from its calling.

I hope that the statue of Eros, wounded and strengthened, will soon be back where it belongs – at the heart of London – and I believe that the wounded and strengthened Church of England will continue to stand where it belongs, in the heart of the villages, towns and cities of our land, offering protection and inspiration to all who gather around it – cracks and all.

If the arguments concerning women priests were fierce, they were not as dangerous to Church unity as the other divisive issue, that of gay priests. The unhappiness to ordain women came mostly from the conservative catholic part of the Church, chiefly because of the damage which might be done to relationships between the Church of England and the Roman Catholic Church. Those with an evangelical Bible-based understanding of the faith had fewer problems because there are a variety of New Testament texts which could be used on both sides of the argument. This is not so with the issue of homosexuality. Few texts in the Bible refer to homosexuality but those which do are all hostile to the practice. For some conservative evangelicals in the Church then the question of homosexuality became a test of whether or not people were being loyal to Bible-based teaching, potentially a Church-fracturing and Communion-dividing question.

I flagged up some of the difficulties which the issue raised for the Church in a 'Thought' in May 1997 shortly before the General Synod was to have one of its many debates on the subject.

GAY? 21 MAY 1997

Good morning. There's a celebration going on in Berlin at the present time: it marks the centenary of the Gay Rights Movement. Now I have to confess that my heart sinks whenever the subject of homosexuality is raised because I know how emotive it is and I know that depending upon what I say I'll get a postbag accusing me either of being oppressive, or lily-livered, or hypocritical, or all three. But the subject won't go away. The House of Bishops did its very best a couple of years ago to produce a report which, though the result of fierce debate and charitable understanding, in the event satisfied nobody totally. The General Synod will be addressing a private member's motion on the subject in July but to be honest I don't think that the outcome will be any more satisfactory. Meanwhile the accusations and counter-accusations will continue to fly around.

The problem is that the Church of England has always sought truth in the Bible, the creeds, and the tradition of the Church, but it also gives a high place to human wisdom as a gift from God. In the case of homosexuality the various truths seem to be in conflict. Wearing my scientific spectacles I am forced to conclude that the evidence is now indicating that homosexuality is part of the natural human condition. Wearing my biblical spectacles I am bound to admit that the Bible, when it addresses the issue at all, is hostile to forms of homosexual practice. So how do we square the circle? Do we go with the scientific evidence and ignore the Bible and so be accused of faithlessly following fashionable trends? Do we stay with biblical and Church tradition and be accused of trampling upon the lives of dedicated Christians? Or do we try to learn more about legitimate biblical interpretation and the human condition by struggling with this intractable issue, knowing that it is going to divide us to the quick? Whatever we do, lives are at stake.

I gain some comfort from a report from somebody not of our tradition, Bernard Levin, when the General Synod was discussing the same issue some years ago. He wrote, 'I saw these good people struggling with an issue that worried and confused them and not coming to any clear conclusions.' 'But on reflection,' he went on, 'to be worried and confused about this and not to come to a clear conclusion is probably the humane thing to do.' Quite.

Following the contributions to the debate and reading around the subject my own position began to change, not basically for human rights reasons, although such reasons are powerful in a Church trying to relate positively to a nation which takes human rights increasingly seriously. But through my own Bible reading I began to have more sympathy with the argument that a faithful, long standing, loving relationship between two people of the same sex may be more akin to the Bible's description of marriage than, say, the serial divorces and remarriages of many in society today. I also reflected upon how the attitude to divorce of Church people and its leaders changed over the decades as people began to have members of their extended family who were divorced and so got a better understanding of the complications involved. Today in the Church of England, not only may a divorced and remarried person be considered for ordination as a priest, but only this year the General Synod discussed whether divorce is an obstacle to a priest becoming ordained as bishop.

The issue of homosexuality became a Communion-fracturing issue in 2004 with the ordination of a practising gay priest, Gene Robinson, as bishop of New Hampshire in America. The primates attempted to hold the Anglican Communion together by designing an 'Anglican Covenant' which in effect would marginalize provinces which followed a similar path to New Hampshire in the future. My 'Thought' of October 2004, 'Danegeld', gave reasons for being unhappy with the covenant proposal.

DANEGELD, 19 OCTOBER 2004

In 991 one of the many battles of the Viking invasion of Britain took place. We have a poet's record of the invaders' message: 'It will be better for you that you should buy off this assault with tribute ... if you are willing to ransom your own people ... you will get in exchange peace and quiet.'

There's been little peace and quiet in the Anglican Communion during the last few years. Depending upon where you stand demands have come for hostages, give up any notion of ordaining gay bishops, or give up all this fundamentalist adherence to literal biblical truth and we will give you in exchange peace and quiet. And the Windsor report, coming from the pen of the archetypal Anglican Archbishop Robin Eames is the latest attempt to achieve some peace and quiet in the Anglican Communion in turbulent times. It's a thoroughly reasonable and reasoned report, seeking to square circles and reconcile the irreconcilable in a mostly non-judgemental and civilized way. The question is, 'does it ask for too many hostages, and will they be forthcoming?'

What are some of those hostages? Expressions of regret on behalf of the American Church at consecrating a practising gay priest whilst not taking sufficient account that it would not be acceptable to large numbers of other Anglicans. But the truth is that however long the American Church had waited, the desire for consensus was just not there. But Eames is even-handed, looking for expressions of regret from those who used wild and sometimes harsh language and weighed into other peoples dioceses without permission from their bishops. But such people believed that they had a duty to bring such aid and comfort to minority conservative congregations hostile to the general climate of their diocese.

Well the hostages may be given and we may win some peace and quiet and the report suggests structures to strengthen the peace and quiet – an agreed covenant spelling out the core of Anglicanism which all Anglican provinces are invited to adopt.

Good proposals, sensible proposals, so why am I left uneasy? Because in its history the Church of England has learned other lessons. The English reformers in the sixteenth century after bloody bouts of mutual persecutions seeking to control the core of the Church came to realize that in the Church of England a wide range of interpretations needed to be allowed in contrast to rigid both Roman Catholic and Protestant thought in which even the smallest details of belief and practice can be regarded as essential parts of an indivisible whole. The genius of Anglicanism was to be Catholic and Reformed, traditional and radical, and it has been in the dynamic of difference held within bonds of respect that truth has been found. Let not that be our hostage, even for the sake of peace and quiet.

Both the divisive issues – women priests and gay priests – were on the agenda when the Archbishop of Canterbury was preparing to pay a visit to the Pope at the end of 2006. I presented a 'Thought' 'They are a Blessing' which pointed to the Church of England's tradition of being a Catholic and Reformed Church but in addition a prophetic Church, developing its life in continuity with Catholic and biblical teachings but trusting that the Holy Spirit may be leading it into fresh ways to engage with the challenges of changing times. The challenge has been to present a changeless message of God's love for God's world so that it hooks into the beliefs and imagination of a world speaking a very different language.

Having spent the bulk of my ministry in the dioceses of Southwark and London, together making up the bulk of Greater London, I was well aware of how metropolitan opinion had dramatically changed on the questions of gender and sex in recent decades, and I had amongst my clergy very many women priests and a number of gay priests. This was no theoretical issue for me. I felt that I had to witness to the fact that these priests were not a problem; they were a blessing.

THEY ARE A BLESSING, 21 NOVEMBER 2006

The Archbishop of Canterbury starts his visit to the Vatican today and the standard story is that progress towards unity between the Roman Catholic Church and the Anglican Communion have been set back, sadly, by the ordination of women as priests and bishops and the fracas concerning gay priests and bishops in the Anglican Church.

There is another way of viewing the same happenings. The Church of England sees itself as being both Catholic and Reformed, taking on many of the reforms of the Reformation Churches whilst keeping a continuity with the Catholic nature of the ordained ministry. More than this, it is possible to judge the Church of England as a prophetic Catholic and Reformed Church, thoughtfully and prayerfully making the developments that the wider Catholic and Orthodox Churches might want to take into their system later.

For example, at the Reformation the Book of Common Prayer offered the people of England, and subsequently people in other lands, worship in their own vernacular language. It took four centuries before the Roman Catholic Church replaced the Latin Mass by local languages as the norm of worship. Again, the Church of England since the Reformation has allowed their clergy to marry. It is only in the last dozen years that the Roman Catholic Church in England has allowed former Anglican priests to become Roman Catholic priests, despite them being married, surely indicating that there is not theological impediment to a married man becoming a priest.

Now we have the development of women being ordained as priests in the Anglican Communion. The decision was taken to ordain them in the belief that this was a legitimate development of Church order. Over 2,000 have already been ordained in the Church of England, and I have 175 ministering in my own diocese. Women now form half the candidates at every ordination. It is nonsensical to believe that there will be any going back – nor should there be. Women priests are not a problem but rather a blessing, not only to the Church of England but to the wider community and I believe to the whole Catholic Church in years to come.

And what of gay priests? Of course there are divisions and splits in the Anglican Communion over this issue at the present time, and because we are a transparent Church, the arguments are conducted in public. But Archbishop and Pope both know that they have serving their respective Churches innumerable dedicated and devoted gay priests, often ministering in the most difficult and dangerous places on earth. They are not a problem. They are a blessing. We may be in the winter of Church unity negotiations, but calling blessings problems is not the way to move towards the spring.

While these theological, but very human disputes were going on in the Church of England, British society was becoming increasingly multicultural in race and faith. This was to bring many challenges for society and the Churches with the danger of groups and communities turning in on themselves. A 'Thought' of May 1988 probes the instinct for human groups, including religious groups, to define themselves in distinction to others and then show hostility to them.

BLUE AND BROWN, 24 MAY 1988

As we all know, Scottish and English football supporters fought at Wembley and last night there were more bombs in Northern Ireland. Then last week we were hearing about clashes between Sikhs and Hindus at the Golden Temple at Amritsar. Why do we behave so badly to one another?

A young teacher at Riceville, Iowa some 25 years ago gave us part of the answer. I have the results on videotape; it really does make compulsive viewing. The children, top juniors, were discussing prejudice. It was all rather cosy and so to make it more realistic the teacher, in all seriousness, told the class that it had been conclusively proved that blue-eyed people were better than those with brown eyes. Brown-eyed people were lazy, careless, dirty and stupid and blue eyed people did well to keep away from them.

The results were dramatic. In the teacher's words, 'Within a few hours, I saw children who had been friends all their lives turn into suspicious and nasty people.' It was as though the blue eyed children had been waiting for years to be told that they were superior, whilst by the end of the brown eyed children looked resentful and cowed.

Next day, the teacher told the class that she'd made a mistake, blue-eyed folk weren't superior, they were inferior. Almost immediately the roles were reversed. Now the brown-eyed children became cocky and confident, performed better in tests and needed little encouragement to taunt their blue-eyed former comrades. Now it was the blue-eyed children's turn to experience resentment and fury.

What stays with me is the ease with which a confident teacher convinced a class of ordinary children of their superiority or inferiority. Nor can I escape by telling myself that these were only children, because a few years later that same teacher performed the same experiment with adult prison warders with very similar results. The truth seems to be that all of us are susceptible to the virus of prejudice.

In a divided society like ours, religion can add to the divisions by building upon our prejudices and focusing upon our differences and fears, or it can hold things together by emphasizing our shared values and beliefs. Most of the world religions teach us that God loves us, not because we are particularly loveable, but because he created us. And that if we're to live happy and harmonious lives we're to treat our neighbour as we would wish to be treated ourselves, for our God created our neighbour too, whether our neighbour's eyes are blue or brown.

In this social mix the question always before us was, 'Is religion going to add to the divisions in British society, or can it be an agent of social cohesion?' During the last two decades faith leaders have worked hard through such agencies as the Inter Faith Network, building upon the work undertaken by local groups to engage in face-to-face dialogue with each other, and also to stand shoulder to shoulder in demonstrating to wider society that religion can be a blessing rather than a problem, a catalyst agent in community building rather than a lever causing division. Local networks continued to be formed and now cover most British cities and regions.

Some Christians have had theological problems about working with those of other faiths. In their mind, with Jesus Christ having a unique position in salvation history, surely the prime duty of the Christian is to convert everyone we meet. But British people have now had the experience of having neighbours of all faiths as fellow citizens and observing that there is much to be admired in all of their dedication and devotion. Many are coming to the conclusion that we all need help in becoming better members of our own faith, that the question of salvation can safely be left to God, and that with the majority of people in Britain having no explicit religious faith, the mission field is hardly empty. We do not need to wave provocative placards on the steps of mosque or temple!

This spirit was well expressed in a *Tablet* leader: 'All the world religions today are challenged to ask each other what they most deeply believe and to see how far they can share, so as to draw strength from each other on behalf of the human family so as to save it from failure.' A former Archbishop of Canterbury, Robert Runcie, gave similar advice to his bishops: 'Strengthen Christians in their faith, defend the rights of those of other faiths, challenge those of no faith.' I believe that this is still good advice and it has formed the background to by own 'Thoughts' on inter-faith matters.

A problem has been the profound ignorance of religion on the part of both national and local politicians and their civil servants. Their default position has been to see religious groups seeking to work for the common good as just another pressure group coming to argue their corner in a self-seeking way. It has been difficult to explain to them that Churches and faiths, as well as undertaking their work of worship and of passing their faith to new generations, want to play their part in the marketplace, working with others for justice, seeking to reduce social conflict, but they do this in a distinctive way, having an accountability to a reality and power beyond the immediate and the local, a power that mostly they would call 'God'.

Marking the millennium was an opportunity for British faith leaders to work together in this way, not only through the design of the 'Faith Pavilion' in the Millennium Dome but in a high-profile ceremony in the Palace of Westminster stressing the gifts which religion brings to society. But there were tensions and some minority faiths in Britain were feeling vulnerable, with 'faith' becoming a code word in public speak for 'Islam'. The events of 9/11 and later 7/7 did not help the situation. The following year the government included an incitement to religious hatred clause within an Anti-terrorism bill. I was involved in the debates on the bill as it made its way through the House of Lords. There were those who felt that this was mistake, not least because the law cannot make people behave in virtuous ways. A counter-argument was that anti-racism legislation had had the effect of making racism in society unacceptable. As recently as 2011 a government minister in the Lords, Baroness Warsi, has claimed that Islamopohobia is the only prejudice now acceptable around Bristish 'dinner tables'.

My argument in the 'Thought' of November 2001 is that not only should we not show hostility to those of different faiths, but in fact we need their experiences, stories and insights, just as they need ours, so that we can better understand ourselves and our values.

RELIGIOUS HATRED, 27 NOVEMBER 2001

This is a good time for religious festivals. Dvalhi, Ramadan, Guru Nanak's Birthday, Christmas and Chanukah are all here or on the horizon. We ought to enjoy our religious celebrations. We ought to know that the great festivals of every faith brings goodness to the whole community. And we ought to remember that this is the real purpose of all our partying.

But things can go wrong. Sometimes, when we celebrate our own faith, we feel that the ways of another faith aren't as good and their celebrations can even seem alien. We want everyone to be the same – and preferably, the same as us! And if they're not this can lead to anger or even hatred.

Yesterday the House of Commons passed the Anti-Terrorism Bill which includes inciting religious hatred as a criminal offence. Of course there will be problems with this. How do you define religion? Will this give protection to some destructive sects who will call themselves religious? Will it question the perfectly legitimate witness which adherents of all faiths wish to make? Such questions will be carefully considered as the bill makes its way through the House of Lords in the next few days. But basically the outlawing of religious hatred is one way of saying that we live in a society of many faiths and that this is a strength not a weakness.

Everywhere we look, we see examples of how life can be improved by difference and variety. Just look at the world of sport. Thirty years ago, all the top players in England were white. Now, the Premier League players are from a wonderful spread of ethnic backgrounds – and the football is very much better, perhaps the best league in the world

It's almost as if we're not complete as human beings unless we get to know those who are different from ourselves. Getting involved with people from different backgrounds, different cultures, different faiths, tells us a whole lot more about what the human race is. It tells us about people who are different from us – but it tells us about us, too. By comparing and contrasting we find out more about who we are and what we stand for, and ultimately who we are and what we stand for before God.

And that, at its heart, is what religion is all about. It gives us the symbols and the rituals, the ways and means to celebrate our past, live brave lives in the present and face the future with hope. The great faiths celebrate Dvalhi, Ramadan, Christmas or Chanukah in a wounded world this year. They play their part in adding to the wounds when they narrowly turn in upon themselves or lash out at a world gone wrong. But they can be part of the key to a world put right, and nowhere do we have a better chance of achieving that than in this tolerant land of ours.

This opportunity of having an experience of other world faiths because they now live next door to us is illuminating in its own right. I was waiting in the queue in my local health centre reading a book by a former BBC Religious Affairs' correspondent, Gerald Priestland's *The Case Against God*. I was conscious of an elderly Asian man next to me using his chain of beads in prayer. After a while he tapped me on the arm and said, 'That is a very bad book.' 'Why do you say that?' I asked. 'It's called *The Case Against God*,' he replied. 'Oh, but that's just the title to get our attention; it's really saying that God is good,' I told him. 'I will never understand you Christians,' he said. I felt that I couldn't leave it there and so I said, 'Well, as we wait you are praying to God in your heart with your beads and I am thinking about God with my mind whilst I read the book.'

He reflected and then said, 'Yes, we call the God in our hearts "Atman".' I said, 'We call the God in our hearts "The Holy Spirit".' He concluded the conversation by saying, 'That is a very good name for God,' and off he went to see the doctor. Probably at no other time in history and at no other place on earth could that inter-faith conversation have taken place in such a natural way, and such conversations not only illuminate the faith of others, but also hold up a mirror to our own, bringing fresh insights and understandings.

But our multi-faith, multicultural network of Churches, mosques, temples, gudwaras and synagogues with their adherents is also a tremendous community resource. I attempted to put some flesh onto the bones of this argument in a 'Thought' presented in May 2002. It points to the innumerable community projects which are faith-based, 3,000 in the 20 poorest boroughs in London alone, 25,000 volunteers providing a service for over 200,000 people. It seems that the 'Big Society' has quietly been at work for over a decade at least, and it is multi-faith in nature.

FAITH COMMUNITY SOCIAL GAIN, 14 MAY 2002

Peter Hain has caused a great deal of comment by remarking that some members of the Muslim community in Britain are isolationist. Well, that cuts both ways. There are parts of this country which are socially polarized by isolationist attitudes. On the other hand, 'Keeping yourself to yourself' has always been a much admired characteristic of the British people, whatever their ethnic origin.

It is also a well-known British axiom that charity begins at home. Such charity often begins in the faith communities but, in my experience, when it's at its best, it doesn't stop there. Take the hundreds of Church of England schools up and down the land. They have places for Christian children, places for the children of other faiths and places for those of no faith. In their environment, our children learn to respect others' traditions.

In London, that really matters. Over 50 religions are practised here and almost 300 languages are spoken. But the many faith communities represented by these numbers are a great blessing. A report published yesterday by the Greater London Enterprise reveals that in the 20 poorest boroughs in London, there are over 3,000 community projects based in faith communities. The projects involve luncheon clubs for the elderly and infirm, mother and toddler clubs and play groups, after school clubs, parenting classes, and drop-in centres and hostels for refugees and asylum seekers. They employ over 4,000 staff, involve more than 25,000 volunteers and provide a service to over 200,000 Londoners.

The social action coming from these faith communities is an expression of God's love for all the citizens of the locality. By it, some of the more battered parts of our land are touched by human compassion and care stemming from divine goodness. The thin morality of the sense of fairness and decency which undergirds national life is strengthened and thickened by a stronger religious motivation – obedience to God's law, love of neighbour, willingness to forgo personal gain for the good of others. Thin morality is strengthened as people are encouraged to move from common ground to higher ground.

Strengthening thin morality, I believe, is answer enough to the question which is often put to religious leaders: 'By what authority do you speak out on social issues?' But the statistics of yesterday's report give a further answer. To use the words of the title of this week's Christian Aid Week, it is the deliberate decision in social terms to 'Choose Hope'. Our faith communities all hold out hope – the hope of God's love for humanity, the hope of a better way forward, the hope of a nobler future. As they display that hope for the communities in which they are set, they can also, here and now, create the better way for which all humanity hopes. Charity, it seems, really does begin at home – in the multicultural Britain which is home to us all and in whose cities we can do better than keep ourselves to ourselves.

The tensions within the Churches, faith communities and society will remain long into the future. In this chapter we have briefly visited some of the most apparent today and we might reflect that they are not merely a challenge but an opportunity for strengthened faith and commitment. The task, now and in the future is, to quote the Dali Lama, to help 'build a world society with a soul'. That is the contribution of religion to the human project. We can do it better together.

Conclusion

What has become evident in the relatively short time that this book has been in preparation is that the world will not keep still and our reflections upon it constantly have to be revised, as previous conclusions are overtaken by new events. Yesterday's wisdom is almost immediately challenged by new realities. Comments on the tsunami of 2004 are partly superseded by the catastrophic earthquake and tsunami in 2011 in Japan; comments on the Gulf wars and Afghanistan come under further challenge by the seeming domino effect of challenges to established regimes in North Africa and the Gulf states, with British armoury marked for redundancy proving to be of significant value in the armed strike against the military force of the Gaddafi regime in Libya; then further changes in government policy illustrate the points made in the chapter on education but might also lead to religious studies virtually disappearing as a separate subject in the curriculum in both schools and colleges.

What is certain is that, with all of this, however well and skilfully leaders in all aspects of public life plan for the future, they will be surprised by unexpected events, and their plans, when put into operation, will have unforeseen consequences.

Religious bodies are not exempt from this law of modern life. We all live and make plans on the frontier between 'what is no longer appropriate' and 'what has not yet been invented'. It is an uncomfortable and demanding place to be, but each of the world faiths have their contribution to make to the mixture. The fundamental religious question is, 'Are there values and truths which are timeless because they come from a transcendent God beyond time, and if so, what are they?'

That question, and the times we live in pose significant issues for faith leaders. Islam has not yet come to terms, theologically and structurally, with being partly immersed in Western countries in post-Enlightenment times. A pertinent question is, 'What is a modern, Westernized Muslim to believe and do?' The post-Christian world of Britain and Western Europe has equally to come to terms with the fact that religion, including Christianity has not disappeared from the Western marketplace, and, if it were to do so, there are hundreds of millions of Christians around the globe for whom religion is the main driving force in their lives. With new generations of young people growing up with idealistic beliefs about ecology, wealth and poverty, peace and justice, liberty and human rights, it seems that the debate about religion and public life still has a long way to run in the public square.